HEROES AND LEGENDS

THOR

BY GRAEME DAVIS
ILLUSTRATED BY MIGUEL COIMBRA

ROSEN
PUBLISHING

New York

Published in 2015 by The Rosen Publishing Group, Inc.
29 East 21st Street, New York, NY 10010

First Edition

Library of Congress Cataloging-in-Publication Data

Davis, Graeme, author.
Thor/Graeme Davis.
    pages cm. — (Heroes and legends)
Reprint of: Long Island City, NY: Osprey Publishing, 2013.
Includes bibliographical references and index.
Audience: Grades 7-12.
ISBN 978-1-4777-8134-0 (library bound)
1. Thor (Norse deity) 2. Mythology, Norse. I. Title.
BL870.T5D38 2015
293'.2113—dc23

2014020519

Manufactured in the United States of America

CONTENTS

INTRODUCTION

Thor is the best known of the Norse gods. From archaeological evidence, he also seems to have been the god favored most by the Vikings themselves. The Vikings identified with Thor in a way they did not with the unpredictable Odin, the unyielding Tyr, and the dangerous Loki.

Thor's popularity can be explained in several ways. As a god of storms and thunder, he would naturally have been important to a society of seafarers, fishermen, and farmers. Literary sources depict Thor as a Viking writ large – strong, bluff, hearty, and fearless – so he may have been something of a role model. He is also fallible: this may be because his adventures were first written down at a time when paganism had given way to Christianity in most of Scandinavia, and contemporary retellings of Norse myths were purged of religious content. This turned them into wild adventure tales and reduced the gods to something like modern superheroes.

Perhaps this is one reason why Thor still makes regular appearances in contemporary culture. Since 1962 he has been one of Marvel Comics' more popular superheroes, appearing in films and television shows as well as in comics. Thor remains a popular boys' name in Scandinavia, and has also been attached to Norwegian and German warships, an American ballistic missile and booster rocket, a British ramjet, and more than one heavy metal act, among other things.

Thor's most popular symbol, the hammer Mjolnir, has been adopted in recent decades by a variety of groups ranging from neopagans to rockers and bikers. In recent years its use has been reported among white supremacists. The swastika, infamously co-opted by the Nazi Party in 1920 and used by racist groups ever since, was also originally associated with Thor. It has been variously interpreted as a stylized thunderbolt or a symbol for Thor's hammer.

This book examines Thor's journey from god to prototypical superhero, and recounts some of the most popular tales told about the Viking god of thunder.

(Opposite) Thor's Fight with the Giants (1872) by Marten Eskil Winge is a typical 19th-century image of the Thunder God. (© National Museum, Stockholm, Sweden / The Bridgeman Art Library)

A NOTE ABOUT SPELLINGS

The primary sources for these tales are not consistent about the spelling of many names. In addition, the Old Norse language features a few letters that are not part of our Roman alphabet, and uses accents above many vowels. The result can be confusing and hard for a modern English-speaker to read. Therefore, character names and poem titles have been simplified in this book for the sake of consistency and readability.

The World of Norse Myth

There are a great many names in this book that may be unfamiliar to the casual reader. In order to avoid confusion, the following pages give a brief summary of the major Norse gods and mythological realms.

The Aesir

The Aesir were one of two tribes of Norse gods. The other, the Vanir, were more obscure and are rarely mentioned in the myths.

Odin was the leader of the Aesir. According to some myths he was the father of Thor and many of the other gods, but this may be a later addition intended to bring Norse mythology into line with the classical Greek and Roman model, where Zeus/Jupiter was the father of the gods as well as their chief. Odin was unpredictable and a cunning magician. While hanging on the world-tree Yggdrasil in what sounds like a shamanic ordeal, he sacrificed an eye in exchange for mystical knowledge. In Norse myths, he often travels among mortals as an old one-eyed man in a broad-brimmed hat, bringing good luck and bad.

Frigga was Odin's wife and the queen of Asgard. She is said to have had the power of prophecy, but little else is said of her.

Loki is a malicious trickster who constantly tries to attack and undermine the Aesir. He is also the father of the goddess Hel, the Midgard Serpent Jormungand, and the great wolf Fenrir, and the mother (through shape-changing) of Odin's eight-legged horse Sleipnir.

Balder, the most beautiful of the Norse gods, is the son of Odin and Frigga. He was killed through Loki's malevolence.

Frey is a Vanir who lives among the Aesir. He and his sister Freyja came to Asgard (along with the little-known Njord, according to some sources) as hostages to seal the peace that ended the Aesir–Vanir war long ago. Both Frey and Freyja seem to be fertility deities.

Tyr was a god of victory in battle, and may also have been the patron deity of the law. When the Aesir determined to bind Fenrir, Tyr placed his hand in the wolf's mouth as a surety that they meant no harm. When Fenrir found himself unable to break the Aesir's bonds, he bit off Tyr's hand.

Sif was Thor's wife. Apart from the fact that her golden hair was much admired, little is known of her.

Heimdall was the watchman of Asgard and would sound the horn Gjallarhorn to raise the alarm when the giants crossed the rainbow bridge Bifrost at the start of Ragnarok, the war at the end of the world.

Various lesser Aesir are mentioned in the mythological sources, but these are the main deities who appear in the tales of Thor's exploits.

(Opposite) An 18th-century Icelandic image of Thor fishing for the Midgard Serpent. (Royal Library, Copenhagen, Denmark / The Bridgeman Art Library)

7

The Nine Worlds

The Nine Worlds of Norse cosmology were arranged around the world-tree Yggdrasil in three layers.

At the top were Asgard, Vanaheim, and Alfheim; in the middle were Midgard, Jotunheim, Svartalfheim, and Nidavellir; and beneath Yggdrasil's roots lay Niflheim and Muspellsheim.

Asgard was the realm of the Aesir, the tribe to which most of the Norse gods belonged. Between Asgard and Midgard stretched Bifrost, the rainbow bridge, guarded by Heimdall against the day when the giants would invade and Ragnarok would begin.

Vanaheim was the home of the Vanir, a second tribe of deities. Apart from Frey, Freyja, and Njord, who lived among the Aesir, the Vanir are obscure. Some scholars suggest that they were the folk-memory of an earlier religion based on the land and fertility.

Alfheim was the land of the Elves (*alfar*). Frey may have had a hall there, or he may have owned a hall called Alfheim, which was situated in Asgard – the myths are unclear.

Midgard was the land of humans. Midgard was encircled by a deep ocean, at the bottom of which lay Jormungand the Midgard Serpent, encircling the world with its tail in its mouth.

Jotunheim was the land of the giants, where many of Thor's adventures take place. It seems to have been much like Midgard.

Svartalfheim was the land of the Dark Elves. Little is said of them in Norse myth, although some scholars equate them with dwarves and claim that Svartalfheim and Nidavellir were two names for the same place.

Nidavellir was the home of the Dwarves. Little else is said of it.

Niflheim was a land of mist and darkness. Ruled by Loki's daughter Hel, it was a land of the dead, inhabited by those who died of disease or old age. Some sources call it Hel after its ruler; others imply that Hel was a separate realm within Niflheim.

Muspellsheim was the land of the fire giants. It was said to be a realm of fire, so hot that no one who was not born there could survive it.

Most of the surviving tales of Thor's adventures are set in Asgard, Midgard, and Jotunheim.

THOR THE LEGEND

Christianity established itself in the Viking homelands of Denmark, Norway, Sweden, and Iceland during the 10th to 13th centuries. The Norse religion was slow to die, especially in remote rural areas, but as elsewhere in Europe, Christianity eventually took over and the older religion was reduced to a collection of rural customs and folklore. But this was not to be the end for Thor and the other Norse gods. In the 13th century, two writers, Saemund Sigfusson and Snorri Sturluson, laid the foundation for almost everything we know today about Norse mythology in the *Eddas*.

Over the centuries that followed, the material in their work has been expanded and adapted for a variety of reasons. Today Thor is a major figure in superhero comics, extremist politics, and revived Norse paganism.

The figure of Thor in the surviving legends is larger than life. He is short-tempered and capable of astounding feats of strength, and his favorite pastime is slaying giants. His approach to any problem is direct and usually violent, except for one story in which he outwits a cunning dwarf to save his daughter. On more than one occasion Loki and other enemies make him look almost foolish, but his strength and fighting prowess see him through every hazard except for his final, fatal battle with the world-encircling Midgard Serpent.

Given these qualities, it is perhaps no surprise that Thor's most visible presence in popular culture is in the guise of a comic-book superhero. In some ways, it could be argued that the Christianized legends of the *Eddas* were the precursors of today's superhero comics.

THORSDRAPA

Thorsdrapa (*The Lay of Thor*) is one of the few sources for Norse myth that predate the *Eddas*. It was composed by 10th-century skaldic poet Eilifr Godrunarson, who served at the court of Norwegian Jarl Haakon Sigurdsson (also called Haakon the Powerful). Although never crowned king, Haakon was the *de facto* ruler of Norway from about 975 to 995.

The poem is hard to read because of its extensive use of *kennings* and other complex language. The main part of the poem tells of Thor's exploits against the giant Geirrod, starting with one of Loki's typical pranks and ending, predictably, with Thor slaughtering giants right and left. The *Thorsdrapa* seems to have been the main source for the poet Snorri Sturluson's retelling.

The *Eddas*

Most of our information on Norse mythology comes from two books, the *Poetic Edda* and the *Prose Edda*. Both were written in Iceland during the 13th century, drawing on earlier sources.

Iceland had adopted Christianity in the year 1000, so the myths were retold without any religious content. Reading between the lines, it is possible to see Thor as a role model for the pagan Vikings who worshiped him: the stories emphasize his strength and fighting prowess, which are put to good use in protecting Asgard from encroaching giants.

The *Poetic Edda*

Attributed to Saemund Sigfusson, the *Poetic Edda* (also known as the *Verse Edda*) comes mainly from a 13th-century manuscript named the *Codex Regius* or *Konungsbok* ("book of kings"), which was rediscovered in 1662. It consists of 32 sections, of which nine contain references to Thor.

Voluspa ("The Prophecy of the Seeress") is an account of the world's beginning and end, as told to Odin by a *volva* or seeress. It includes a detailed account of Ragnarok, the war at the end of the world in which Thor and the other gods are destined to be killed.

Grimnismal ("The Sayings of Grimnir") is mainly a story about Odin, but includes an account of the gods and the worlds of Norse myth.

Skirnismal ("The Sayings of Skirnir") mentions Thor fleetingly as one of the gods who will be angry with a giantess who rejects the advances of a lovesick Frey.

Harbardsljod ("The Lay of Harbard") features Thor as a main character. While returning to Asgard from Jotunheim, the land of the giants, Thor encounters an uncooperative ferryman (who may be Odin in disguise, according to some scholars) and the two engage in a *flyting* match, an exchange of poetic insults. Several of Thor's exploits are mentioned in the course of the argument.

Hymiskvida ("Hymir's Poem") sees Thor visiting the giant Hymir to borrow a cauldron large enough to heat mead for all the gods at once. Along the way Thor performs several feats of strength, kills a number of giants, and almost catches the world-encircling Midgard Serpent while fishing.

Thor (1844), a marble statue by B. E. Fogelberg. (Ivy Close Images / Alamy)

Lokasenna ("Loki's Quarrel") tells of a feast at which the trickster god Loki insults all of the gods, and only agrees to leave after Thor threatens to knock his head off with his great hammer Mjolnir.

Thrymskvida ("The Tale of Thrym") tells how the giant Thrym steals Thor's hammer and refuses to return it unless he is allowed to marry the goddess Freyja. Thor and Loki go to Thrym's hall disguised as a bride and bridesmaid; when the hammer is laid in the bride's lap as part of the wedding ceremony, Thor kills the giants with it.

Alvissmal ("The Talk of Alvis") is a dialogue between Thor and a dwarf named Alvis ("all-wise") who comes to claim Thor's daughter as his bride. Thor refuses since he was not consulted about the match, and the rest of the poem is a contest of questions and answers between the two, mainly concerning the different names by which men, Aesir, elves, dwarves, giants, and others call various things.

Hyndluljod ("The Lay of Hyndla") concerns the quest of the goddess Freyja and the seeress Hyndla to establish the pedigree of Freyja's protégé Ottar the Simple, so he can come into his inheritance. Thor is mentioned only in passing.

A 19th-century woodcut image of Snorri Sturluson by Christian Krohg. (PD-US)

Snorri Sturluson and the *Prose Edda*

Snorri Sturluson (1179-1241) was an Icelandic poet and politician. Although he reached the highest office in the land, that of *logsogumadur* (lawspeaker) of Iceland's Althing parliament, he is best known today for having written the *Prose Edda* and the *Heimskringla*.

The *Heimskringla* is a history of the kings of Norway, and its only mythological content is found in the *Ynglinga Saga*, which covers the period from the dawn of time until the rule of Halfdan the Black in the 9th century. The *Prose Edda*, on the other hand, is a collection of Norse legend and history that constitutes one of the two major extant sources for Norse mythology.

The *Prose Edda* (also known as the *Younger Edda*) consists of a prologue and three chapters: *Gylfaginning, Skaldskaparmal,* and *Hattatal.*

SOURCES FOR THE *EDDAS*

The *Codex Regius* ("king's manuscript"), the main source for the *Verse Edda,* was discovered in the 17th century, when the bishop of Skalholt in Iceland sent it as a gift to King Frederick III of Denmark: it was at this time that it acquired its name. It remained in the Royal Library in Copenhagen until 1971, when it was returned to Iceland. It is written on vellum, and 45 leaves survive; eight went missing at some point in its history.

Confusingly, one of the main sources for the *Prose Edda,* sent to Frederick as part of the same gift, is also called the *Codex Regius*. It consists of 55 vellum leaves, and was returned to Iceland in 1985.

Not all of the *Eddas'* content is found in the *Codex Regius*, and scholars have worked to reassemble what they can from many other manuscripts.

Prologue

The Prologue is an attempt to tie the origins of Norse myth into the classical world of Greece and Rome. This was a common exercise among the historians of northern and western Europe at a time when the classical world was regarded as the fount of all civilization and culture. The English historian Geoffrey of Monmouth (*c.* 1100-1155), for example, claims in his *Historia Regum Britanniae* ("History of the Kings of Britain") that Britain's first king was a Roman named Brutus, whose descent he traces back to Troy and the Greek gods.

For his part, Snorri claims that Thor was a grandson of Priam, the last Trojan king from Homer's *Iliad*. He goes on to make Odin Thor's grandson. Thor's descendants make their way to Scandinavia and are welcomed as "men of Asia," which is how Snorri explains the origin of the Norse term *Aesir*.

Gylfaginning

Gylfaginning ("The Tricking of Gylfi") is a story of about 20,000 words, and deals with the beginning and the end of the world according to Norse myth.

The chapter takes its name from Gylfi, a king of Sweden who welcomes the Aesir to Scandinavia in the Prologue. The story begins when Gylfi is tricked by an Aesir goddess, and wonders whether all Aesir use magic and trickery.

HIGH, JUST-AS-HIGH, AND THIRD

The nature of these three figures is never made clear in the *Gylfaginning*. Since Gylfi is traveling to Asgard, though, they may be gods in disguise. Many Norse temples seem to have had three idols – Odin, Thor, and Frey – sitting together. Perhaps High, Just-as-High, and Third are these gods under false names. Most Norse gods had multiple names, and Odin in particular was fond of using aliases.

Gylfi questions the three strangers in *Gylfaginning*. From an 18th-century Icelandic manuscript in the Arni Magnusson Institute in Iceland. (PD-US)

KENNINGS

Kennings are a poetic device popular in Norse literature. They are basically metaphors that use the form "X of the Y" (or the simpler "Y-X") in place of a single noun. Thus, a *kenning* for a ship might be "wave-serpent," referring to a dragon-shaped stem and to the vessel's deadliness in battle.

The most admired *kennings* were derived from Norse myth and literature. For example, a *kenning* for gold was "Sif's hair," referring to a myth in which Loki cut off Sif's hair as a cruel joke, and the dwarves made her new hair out of gold. The more obscure and original a *kenning* was, the more the speaker or writer would be admired.

The most common *kenning* referring to Thor was "giant-slayer." His fondness for fighting giants will be seen in a later chapter.

Determined to find out, Gylfi sets out for Asgard, but is tricked along the way and finds himself in a great palace where three men (named High, Just-as-High, and Third) challenge him to show his wisdom by questioning them. The questions he asks are about the gods and the world's beginning and end, and the answers of these three mysterious strangers make up most of the chapter's text.

Skaldskaparmal

Skaldskaparmal ("The Language of Poetry") is a chapter of about 50,000 words and takes the form of a dialogue between Aegir, the god of the sea, and Bragi, the god of poetry. The two discuss the finer points of poetic style, and along the way Bragi gives the origins of a number of *kennings*, many of which owe their origins to myths and legends.

Hattatal

Hattatal ("List of Verse-Forms") is a chapter of about 20,000 words. It is a poem of praise in traditional skaldic style lauding King Hakon Hakonarson of Norway (1204-63) and his co-regent and future father-in-law Earl Skuli (1188/9-1240) for their generosity and valor. It exemplifies a wide variety of 13th-century Norse verse-forms and is accompanied by a prose commentary that points out the main features of each verse-form.

Hattatal contains no significant mythological content.

How Thor got his Hammer

This tale from the *Skaldskaparmal* tells how the great magical hammer named Mjolnir came to Thor as a result of one of Loki's pranks. Thor's wife, the earth-goddess Sif, was renowned for the beauty of her golden hair until one day Loki cut it off in a fit of mischief. Thor was so angry that Loki feared for his life, and promised to make good the damage he had caused. Being Loki, of course, he could not do it without playing a prank on someone else.

A group of dwarves called the Sons of Ivaldi had made several great magical treasures for the Aesir. These included Odin's spear Gungnir, which never missed its target, and Frey's magical ship Skidbladnir, which always had a following wind and was large enough to carry all the Aesir, despite the fact that Frey could fold it up like cloth and carry it in his pouch.

Sindri creates Mjolnir while Brokk is tormented by Loki in the form of a fly. Arthur Rackham, 1901. (PD-US)

Loki persuaded these talented dwarves to make new hair for Sif out of pure gold, and they succeeded. Not only did Sif's new hair look real, but it also grew like natural hair. Then Loki saw an opportunity for further mischief.

He approached two more dwarves, a pair of brothers called Brokk and Sindri, and bet them that they could not create anything to compete with these wonders. He offered them his own head as a wager, and they accepted eagerly.

To make sure he would not lose the bet, Loki turned himself into a fly and buzzed around the brothers' forge, biting them to distract them from their work. Despite being stung on the hand, Brokk was able to keep the bellows working without a stop until Sindri had made a magical boar named Gullinbursti ("Golden Bristles"). Gullinbursti could run through air and over water, and its golden hide was so bright that it banished darkness wherever it went. Gullinbursti was presented to the god Frey and pulled his chariot.

THOR'S TREASURES

According to myth, Thor owned a number of magical treasures:

The magical hammer Mjolnir ("Crusher") was made by the dwarves Brokk and Sindri, who also made the most of the Norse gods' other magical treasures. It was a fearsome weapon, capable of flattening mountains. When he threw it, Mjolnir never failed to strike its target, and always flew back to his hand. When Thor wanted, Mjolnir could become so small that he could keep it inside his tunic. The tale repeated here is the only place in Norse myth that refers to Mjolnir being short in the handle, and it seems that this reference was only put in for the sake of the story: on his third attempt to distract the dwarves from their task, Loki manages to ruin one item in a small way. Otherwise the hammer is depicted at various sizes.

The belt Megingjord ("Belt of Power") doubled Thor's strength, which was already prodigious. The gloves Jarngreipr ("Iron Gripper") allowed Thor to wield Mjolnir. It is not clear whether the gloves gave Thor the necessary strength, or whether they were needed for some other reason.

In some stories, Thor rode in a chariot pulled by two magical goats, Tanngrisnir ("Teeth-barer") and Tanngnjostr ("Teeth-grinder"). Thor could kill and eat them, using the power of Mjolnir to resurrect them for the next day's travel. In one story, the child of a peasant family with whom Thor shared a goat dinner broke one of their bones to suck out the marrow; as a result, one of the goats (the story does not say which) was left permanently lame.

Sindri put some more gold in the brothers' furnace and told Brokk to keep working the bellows. Determined to keep his head, Loki remained in his fly form and bit Brokk twice on the neck. Brokk kept working the bellows, however, and Sindri used the gold to make a gold ring called Draupnir ("dripper"), which was presented to Odin. Draupnir had the magical property of creating, or "dripping" from itself eight gold rings of equal weight on every ninth night.

The brothers kept working, fashioning a mighty hammer (although some sources refer to Mjolnir as an axe or a club). Loki bit Brokk again, this time on the eye, and he stopped working the bellows for a moment. As a result, Mjolnir was a little short in the handle, which is why Thor needed the magical iron gloves Jarngreipr to wield it. Mjolnir's magic was such that it would never miss a target at which it was thrown, and it would always return to the thrower's hand.

Even with its short handle, the Aesir all agreed that the hammer was the best of all their treasures. They decided that this mighty weapon belonged in the hands of their mightiest warrior, and it was given to Thor.

Having lost his wager with Brokk and Sindri, Loki tried to flee. Thor caught him and handed him over to the dwarves so that they could collect their due by cutting off the trickster's head. However, they were thwarted when Loki argued that they could not cut off his head without harming his neck, and his neck was not part of the wager. The two dwarves contented themselves with sewing the trickster's mouth shut.

THOR AND UTGARDALOKI

This long tale is told in *Gylfaginning*. Thor shows his usual strength and determination, but they do him little good in the face of an opponent who is both wily and magical. Utgardaloki humbles Thor in a variety of ways, casting doubt upon his strength at every turn until in the end it is revealed that the Thunder God has been the victim of a series of illusions. His strength and prowess are still unsurpassed; only in the face of trickery is he powerless.

In talking with the three mysterious figures he meets in Asgard, Gylfi asks whether Thor has ever been defeated. One of them responds by telling the following tale:

Thjalfi and Roskva

Thor and Loki were traveling together and stopped at a farm for the night. To repay the farmer's hospitality, Thor killed his goats and made a stew. The farmer's son, whose name was Thjalfi, cracked one of the bones to eat the marrow, and when Thor used the magic of Mjolnir to resurrect his goats the following morning, he found that one of them was lame.

Thor's scowl at this discovery so frightened the farmer and his family that they offered him Thjalfi and his sister Roskva as servants. Thjalfi remained in the Thunder God's service from then on, but Roskva is hardly mentioned.

The Giant Skrymir

Leaving the goats behind, Thor and his companions traveled into Jotunheim. Passing through a great forest, they looked for a place to spend the night, and at last they came upon a great hall and went inside. The hall was empty, but about midnight they were disturbed by a terrible earthquake and took refuge in a small side-chamber. Thor stood guard over the entrance, his hammer in his hand. For the rest of the night, a great moaning and roaring kept the companions awake.

When dawn came, the group emerged from the hall to find a giant sleeping not far from the building. He was snoring very loudly, and Thor realized that this was the noise they had heard during the night. He put on his strength-boosting belt Megingiord just as the man awoke. As he stood up it was clear he was a giant of immense size, and for once Thor was not prepared to strike him down.

(Opposite) Thor wrestles with an old woman named Elli, who turns out to be old age personified.

The giant said his name was Skrymir ("Big Fellow"), and asked what Thor had done with his glove. Thor and his companions were puzzled until Skrymir reached out and picked up the hall where the travelers had spent the night. It was an immense glove, and the side-chamber where they had taken refuge was the thumb.

After he had put his glove back on, Skrymir asked the companions if he could travel with them, and they agreed. Skrymir offered to carry all the group's provisions, and the others put their food in his sack.

The following night, while Skrymir was asleep, Thor tried to open his sack to get something to eat, but could not loosen the strings at all. In his frustration,

Thor fearlessly walked up to this strange monster to have a better look at him.

Thor encounters Skrymir in this 1930s book illustration by Charles Edmund Brock. (The Bridgeman Art Library)

Thor grasped his hammer Mjolnir and aimed a mighty blow at Skrymir's head. The giant woke up and asked mildly if a leaf had fallen on his head.

Skrymir went back to sleep, but his snoring kept Thor and the others awake. Thor struck him another blow with his hammer, this time so hard that Mjolnir's head sank deep into the giant's crown. Skrymir awoke again and asked if an acorn had fallen on him. Thor retreated and waited for Skrymir to go back to sleep.

Shortly before daybreak, Thor saw that Skrymir was asleep again. He struck him another blow, sinking Mjolnir up to its handle into the giant's temple. Skrymir sat up and rubbed his head, asking if there was a bird in the branches above him that might have dislodged a piece of moss.

Since the sun was already rising, Skrymir suggested that the group should travel on. There was a hall named Utgard that was not too far off. Before they got there, he warned his companions to be careful of their manners; they might think he was big, but he was quite small compared to Utgard's ruler, Utgardaloki, and his servants. Thor and the others were puny by comparison, and it would be dangerous for them if they caused offense. As for himself, he would continue his journey to the north. He parted company with the rest of the group and set off.

Utgard

Thor and his companions journeyed on till noon, when they arrived at a vast fortress. Even with his Aesir strength, Thor was unable to open the huge gate that guarded the entrance, and the travelers were forced to squeeze between its bars.

They went to Utgardaloki and greeted him courteously, but he treated them with contempt. He made some disparaging comments about Thor's small stature, and told the companions that no one could stay in Utgard unless they proved themselves capable of some superhuman feat.

Quick-witted Loki stepped forward and boasted that no one could eat faster than he could. Utgardaloki smiled and ordered a meat-filled trough set up on the floor. Loki was stationed at one end, and at the other sat one of Utgardaloki's servants, whose name was Logi. Food was brought in, and the two began to eat. They ate their way along the trough until they met exactly in the middle. Even so, Loki lost the contest. While he had eaten all the meat in his half of the trough, his opponent had eaten the meat, the bones, and the trough itself.

Utgardaloki turned to Thor's servant Thjalfi, and asked what he could do. Thjalfi answered that he would try a foot race against anyone his host might choose. Utgardaloki summoned another of his servants, whose name was Hugi, and led the company to a flat plain outside the fortress.

The race was run in three heats. In the first heat, Hugi was barely ahead of Thjalfi when he turned at the halfway point. Hugi admitted that he had never met anyone who was faster than Thjalfi. In the second heat, however,

Thor tries to lift Utgardaloki's cat, which is actually the Midgard Serpent magically disguised. An unattributed book illustration from 1872. (PD-US)

Thjalfi lagged behind by a bow-shot when Hugi reached the turning point. In the third, Thjalfi had not reached the middle of the course by the time Hugi turned around. Everyone agreed that Hugi was the winner.

Now Utgardaloki turned to Thor and asked him what feat he wished to display. Thor chose a drinking contest, and an ale-horn was brought in. It was not unusually large, although Thor did notice that it seemed very long. Utgardaloki challenged Thor to empty the horn in a single draught. Some men took two draughts, he said, but even the poorest drinker could empty it in three.

Thor raised the horn and swallowed until his breath gave out, but the horn seemed no less full than when he had started. Utgardaloki told him he had expected better from all the tales he had heard of Thor's exploits, and invited him to drink a second draught. Thor raised the horn and drank again, but did no better than before. Utgardaloki chided him, asking if he had overestimated his ability by leaving more for the third draught than he could manage. Worse, he wondered aloud if Thor's reputation had been exaggerated.

Stung by this, Thor drank with all his might, but although the level was visibly lower he was still unable to empty the drinking horn. Utgardaloki observed that Thor's might was not as great as he had supposed, but offered him the chance of another challenge if he wished to take it. Thor countered that among the Aesir such a drink would not be considered small, and said that he was ready to accept any other challenge.

Utgardaloki pointed out a sleeping cat and challenged Thor to lift it. He said that the young men of Utgard did such things for sport; he would not have offered Thor such a puny challenge if he had not already seen that Thor's strength was far less than he had previously believed.

The cat was gray and rather large, but Thor grabbed it around the middle and tried to lift it up. Although he was able to raise the cat's middle, its paws stayed on the floor. Thor stretched as high as he could and finally one paw left the ground, but that was as much as he could do. Utgardaloki admitted that the cat was rather large, and pointed out that Thor was rather small by the standards of Utgard.

Mad with frustration by now, Thor retorted that whatever his size might be, he was ready to wrestle with anyone who dared take him on. Utgardaloki looked around at the benches where his servants were seated, and mused that it would be hard to find anyone who would regard a wrestling match with Thor as any kind of challenge. Finally he called upon his foster-mother, an old woman named Elli, and bade her wrestle with the Thunder God.

Thor took hold of Elli and tried to grapple with her, but the tighter his hold the firmer she seemed to stand. They stood deadlocked. Then Elli moved slightly and Thor lost his footing. They wrestled for a long time, but finally Elli was able to force Thor down onto one knee.

Utgardaloki stopped the bout and declared that it was time to eat. For the rest of the evening, the visitors enjoyed the best of hospitality.

The Truth Revealed

The following morning, Utgardaloki provided his visitors with the best of breakfasts and sent them on their way. Before they left, however, he spoke to Thor, asking if he had ever before met anyone who was stronger than he was. Thor admitted that he had been humiliated and embarrassed by his experience in Utgard. Utgardaloki said that he would now tell Thor the truth, since he did not expect Thor ever to return to Utgard. Indeed, he said, he would never have permitted Thor to enter his hall if he had known how strong he truly was.

Firstly, said Utgardaloki, the giant Skrymir with whom the companions had traveled was Utgardaloki himself, in disguise. Thor could not open Skrymir's sack because he had tied it with iron bands and made sure that Thor could not find them. When Thor struck three times at Skrymir's head, Skrymir had woven an illusion that made Thor hit a nearby mountain instead; the mountain was now cloven by three square valleys, each deeper than the last.

Next Utgardaloki explained why his visitors had lost their contests with his servants. Logi, to whom Loki lost the eating contest, was really Wildfire, which consumes everything in its path with frightening speed. Hugi, who beat Thjalfi in the foot race, was actually Thought, and nothing is swifter than thought.

Finally, Utgardaloki revealed the truth behind Thor's three challenges.

Thor was unable to drain the drinking horn because its far end was in the sea. Although Thor could not drink up all the oceans, he had drunk enough to lower the waters to ebb tide. Utgardaloki admitted that he had never thought such a feat was possible.

The large gray cat that Thor had failed to lift up was actually the world-encircling Midgard Serpent, disguised by another of Utgardaloki's illusions. When Thor picked it up his hands almost reached the stars, and the Midgard Serpent's head and tail almost left the ground.

Elli, the old woman who had wrestled Thor to one knee, was none other than Old Age itself, which overcomes everyone in the end.

Having revealed his deceptions, Utgardaloki warned Thor never to return, promising that he would defend Utgard with equally powerful illusions if the Thunder God ever troubled him.

Enraged by Utgardaloki's duplicity, Thor raised his hammer to strike him down, but the giant was no longer there. Thor turned toward Utgard, intending to batter it to rubble, but the fortress had also vanished, leaving only a beautiful but empty plain.

In frustration, Thor returned to his hall at Thrudvang. He never forgot his humiliation at Utgardaloki's hands, though, and he promised himself a reckoning against the giants and against the Midgard Serpent itself.

An image of Thor from an 18th-century Icelandic manuscript. (PD-US)

GIANTS AND TROLLS

Today, thanks largely to the influence of *Dungeons & Dragons* and other fantasy games, giants and trolls are regarded as very different creatures. In Norse myth, however, the words "giant" and "troll" seem to have been synonymous – indeed there are instances where both words are used to describe the same creature.

In post-Viking folklore, trolls can be almost any size and their appearance and other characteristics are extremely various. In modern Danish the word *trolddom* means magic in general, and the phrase "*svaerd og trolddom*" has the same meaning as the English "sword and sorcery."

AEGIR'S FEAST

Aegir (not to be confused with the Aesir, the divine tribe of which Thor is a member) is a slightly enigmatic figure in Norse mythology. Some scholars regard him as a god of the ocean, while others see him as a powerful giant who lived beneath the sea.

This legend is found partly in *Lokasenna* and partly in *Hymiskvida*. Another version, told in *Gylfaginning*, covers only the fishing expedition and states that Thor visits Hymir in the guise of a mortal youth, disguising his strength and divine power.

The story of Thor's catching the Midgard Serpent is represented in several sources that are older than the *Eddas*. The 9th-century *Ragnarsdrapa* includes a version of the tale, as do the 10th-century *Husdrapa* and fragments of two other 10th-century poems. In the first two cases, the poets describe not the event itself, but representations of it on a shield (which, since it is also said to bear images from three other legends, must be nothing more than a narrative device) and in the carvings of a hall owned by a wealthy Icelandic merchant.

Images of Thor hooking Jormungand can be found on several carved stones from the Viking Age, including a 10th-century cross in St. Mary's churchyard at Gosforth in the English county of Cumbria.

A part of the Gosforth Cross, showing Thor fishing for the Midgard Serpent. (PD-US)

Thor Hooks the Midgard Serpent

The Aesir visited Aegir and he prepared a feast for them. Aegir was famed for the number and size of his cauldrons, and when they saw them the Aesir decided that Aegir should host all their gatherings in future.

Aegir could not refuse them without being a bad host, but he set one condition that the Aesir should provide him with a cauldron large enough to warm mead for all of them at once. Even among such a collection of cauldrons as he possessed, there was no vessel large enough to do so. Tyr, the god of the law, remembered that his father Hymir owned a vessel that was no less than a *rast* (about 7 miles)

Hymir cuts Thor's fishing line in this 1901 illustration by Arthur Rackham. (PD-US)

deep, which would answer Aegir's need perfectly. Tyr and Thor set out to bring this huge cauldron back to Aegir's hall.

When the two gods arrived at Hymir's steading, they were confronted at first by Tyr's grandmother, an ugly giantess with nine hundred heads. Then Tyr's mother came out, "all-golden" and "fair-browed," and offered a cup of ale to her son. She warned the two gods to hide under Hymir's cauldrons, saying that he was often ill-disposed to receiving guests.

When Hymir returned from hunting, they found that Tyr's mother had been right. His beard was crusted with ice, and the icebergs cracked under his fierce gaze. When Tyr's mother told him that he had visitors, Hymir's glance

(Overleaf) Thor battles the world-encircling Midgard Serpent Jormungand.

Thor struggles with the Midgard Serpent while Hymir prepares to cut the line. W. G. Collingwood, 1908. (PD-US)

shattered one of the hall's pillars, sending cauldrons crashing to the floor and breaking all but one.

Although Hymir was not pleased to see that one of his visitors was the renowned giant-slayer Thor, he grudgingly offered the two his hospitality. He ordered three oxen to be slaughtered for a feast. Thor ate two of them by himself. It was agreed that on the next day, they would be forced to eat whatever they could catch. Sent to find bait, Thor cut off the head of Hymir's best ox and carried it to Hymir's boat.

The three rowed out to Hymir's favorite fishing spot, but Thor insisted on heading into deeper waters in search of a better catch. Hymir caught two whales, but then Thor fastened the ox head to a line and threw it overboard. Almost immediately, he hooked the largest creature in the sea: Jormungand, the world-encircling Midgard Serpent.

Jormungand fought with all its immense strength, but Thor would not let go of his line, even when the Midgard Serpent pulled him through the bottom of the boat. Bracing his feet against the ocean floor, Thor hauled Jormungand up to the side of the boat.

As the Midgard Serpent towered above their vessel, venom spewing from its jaws, Thor prepared to strike out at it with his hammer. Before he could do so, however, a panicked Hymir cut the line and released the mighty beast. In a rage, Thor threw his hammer at the Serpent, striking it in the head but apparently not killing it. Then, he turned his frustration on Hymir and struck him on the side of the head with his hand. The force of the blow flung the giant from the boat, and Thor waded back to shore.

Once the whales had been brought in and they were eating, Hymir insulted Thor's strength, saying that the Thunder God could not even break Hymir's wine cup. Thor dashed the cup against a stone. The stone split in two, but the cup remained intact. Thor was baffled until Tyr's mother advised him to break the cup against Hymir's head. He did so, and the cup shattered.

After this, Hymir agreed to let the Aesir have the cauldron they asked for, if they could take it out of his hall. Tyr tried twice, but could not even lift it. Thor grasped the vessel by the rim and tried to lift it up, but its weight forced him through the floor. Finally he managed to raise the cauldron onto his head, and they set off for Aegir's hall.

Hymir was not willing to let the Aesir go so easily. He pursued them with "a troop of many-headed monsters," but Thor set down the cauldron and threw his hammer Mjolnir at their pursuers, killing all of them including Hymir. Then the two gods returned in triumph to Aegir's hall, bearing the gigantic cauldron.

Loki's Insult

This tale, recounted in *Lokasenna*, continues the previous story.

When Thor and Tyr returned with Hymir's cauldron, Aegir brewed enough ale for all the Aesir. Thor was absent, but the other gods all assembled for the feast. Among them was the troublemaking Loki, who was in a foul mood because the Aesir had recently bound Loki's offspring Fenrir (also known as Fenris), a gigantic wolf who according to prophecy would kill Odin at Ragnarok.

Aegir's servants Fimafeng and Eldir welcomed the Aesir to the hall. The gods were impressed by how well these two attended to their duties, and Loki grew so tired of hearing their praise that he killed Fimafeng. As a result, he was banished from the feast. Encountering Eldir a little while later, Loki asked what the Aesir were talking about. Eldir answered that the gods were discussing their might at arms, and added that no one had a kind word for Loki.

Enraged, Loki went back into Aegir's hall, demanding hospitality according to custom. Bragi, the god of poetry, told Loki once more that he was unwelcome. After Loki reminded Odin of an oath that he and Loki would drink together, Odin reluctantly told his son Vidar to give up his place to the trickster god. Vidar did so, and even poured a drink for Loki.

Taking the drink, Loki offered a toast to all the assembled gods, pointedly excluding Bragi. Bragi responded by offering Loki a horse, a ring, and a sword to mend things between them, but Loki rejected the gifts, accusing Bragi of cowardice for offering them. Bragi responded to Loki's insult by saying that he would have taken Loki's head if it were not for the fact that they were under the peace of Aegir's hall. Loki insulted Bragi's courage again, saying that he was brave enough while he stayed in his seat.

When the goddess Idun tried to intercede, Loki accused her of having loose morals. He went on to insult all the gods in turn, pouring his malice upon everyone who spoke to him. He accused the goddess Gefion of immorality as well, and when Odin protested he claimed that he gave victory to cowards and criticized him for traveling among mortals in disguise rather than admitting his identity.

Odin's wife Frigga tried to quell the argument, but Loki dismissed her as having always been too fond of men. Wounded, Frigga replied that she would not have to suffer such insults if her son Balder were still alive, prompting Loki to gloat about his part in Balder's death.

Freyja, the goddess of love and fertility, now tried to calm Loki, but he shot back that there was no man in Aegir's hall who had not been her lover. When she protested at his insults, Loki went further. She was a witch, he said, and had even slept with her own brother Frey.

Freyja and Frey's father, the Vanir god Njord, now objected. Loki reminded him that he had come to Asgard as a hostage to secure peace after a long-ago Aesir-Vanir war, and accused him of improper relations with giantesses. When Njord told Loki that he was glad he had a son whom no one hated (unlike Loki, who had fathered Fenrir and the Midgard Serpent), Loki retorted that Njord had got his son and his daughter through incest with his own sister.

Tyr came to Frey's defense, but Loki cut him down by saying that the law-god was impotent to settle any quarrel. He also reminded him of his missing hand, which Fenrir had torn from him when the Aesir tricked him. Tyr replied that he would rather be missing his hand than his reputation, and noted that Fenrir was bound up until Ragnarok. Loki responded to this by pointing out that he had other sons – including, he claimed, one by Tyr's wife.

Frey stepped in at this point, threatening Loki that he would be bound up like Fenrir if he did not be quiet. Loki noted that Frey would have no sword at Ragnarok, and claimed that he had traded it to the giant Gymir to buy his daughter Gerd for a wife.

Byggvir now addressed Loki. He is an obscure deity, not known outside this one story: his name may be related to the Old Norse word for barley. He said that if he were of Frey's race he would crush Loki, but Loki dismissed him, accusing him of cowardice: "lying in thy truckle bed, thou wast not to be found while men were fighting."

When Heimdall accused Loki of being drunk, Loki responded that he was of no account since he was just a watchman. When the goddess Skadi objected, Loki claimed she had once taken him to her bed.

Thor's wife Sif offered Loki a drink to restore the peace, begging him not to tarnish her reputation. Loki called her an adulteress, claiming that she once betrayed her husband with Loki himself.

At this point Thor returned from whatever journey had kept him from arriving with the rest of the Aesir. He threatened to knock Loki's head off with his hammer, but Loki was unimpressed, pointing out that Thor would be unable to save his father Odin from the jaws of Fenrir at Ragnarok.

Thor threatened Loki again, promising to knock him "into the east region" (possibly meaning all the way to Jotunheim), where no one would ever see him again. Loki laughed, reminding Thor how he had once cowered in the thumb of Utgardaloki's glove.

Thor threatened Loki a third time, saying that Mjolnir would break every bone in his body. Loki reminded him of another of his misadventures with Utgardaloki, when he was too weak to open the food sack belonging to the giant Skrymir.

Finally, Thor threatened to hit Loki so hard that he would be cast down to Hel. At this Loki finally agreed to leave, but not without a parting shot. Aegir, he prophesied, would never host another gathering: fire would take his hall and all his possessions.

Vidar kills Fenrir, avenging his father Odin at the final battle of Ragnarok. W. G. Collingwood, 1908. (PD-US)

THOR AND THE GIANTS

Utgardaloki was not the only giant who crossed Thor's path, though he seems to have been the only one to get the better of the Thunder God. According to the *Eddas*, fighting giants was Thor's favorite pastime. Their enormous size and strength seems to have made them the only foes he considered worthy. His exploits against the giants were so well known that "giant-slayer" was a commonly used *kenning* referring to him.

This chapter relates a few of his better-known exploits against the giants.

Thor's Duel with Hrungnir

This tale from the *Skaldskaparmal* is typical of Thor's exploits against the giants. It stresses both their great size and their ill manners, while emphasizing Thor's strength and prowess in battle. The oldest known version of the tale is in a 10th-century poem called *Haustlong*, which describes an image from the story painted onto a shield.

The story begins when Odin is riding through Jotunheim, one of the giant realms, on his eight-legged horse Sleipnir. He met with a giant named Hrungnir ("the Brawler"), who admired Sleipnir but boasted that his own horse Goldfax ("Gold-mane") had a longer stride.

Odin wagered his head that no horse in Jotunheim could match Sleipnir, and Hrungnir leaped onto Goldfax and chased after him. The race ended at

(Opposite) Thor disguises himself as a bride to get his hammer back from the giant Thrym.

THE GIANTS

Jotunheim lies to the east of Asgard, and its inhabitants, beside being immense of stature, are usually crude, violent, and envious of all that the Aesir possess. Their names bear out their character: Hrungnir ("Brawler"), Thrym ("Uproar"), Thrivaldi ("Thrice Mighty"), Angrboda ("Grief-bringer"), and so on.

Most Jotuns are human-looking, but a few are not. Thrivaldi had nine heads (all of which, according to a passing mention in the *Skaldskaparmal*, Thor clove apart), while Thjazi scarcely ever appears in humanoid form, preferring that of a giant eagle.

Thor's fondness for slaying giants is more than a love of battle and a search for worthy opponents, although these are certainly powerful motives. By killing giants on their own territory, he is discouraging them from coming to Asgard and causing trouble, thus protecting not only Asgard itself but the mortal realm of Midgard beyond it.

the gates of Asgard with Odin still in the lead. When they arrived, Odin invited Hrungnir into his hall of Valhalla.

Freyja and the other goddesses served Hrungnir with mead. He drank bowl after bowl, and as he became drunk his boasting increased. Admiring Odin's hall, Hrungnir said that he would move it to Jotunheim and live in it himself. First he would have to kill all the Aesir, except for Freyja and Sif, Thor's wife, whom he would take with him.

Eventually the Aesir tired of their ill-mannered guest, and called Thor. He scowled to see a giant slumped half-drunk in Odin's hall and demanded to know what right Hrungnir had to be there. Hrungnir replied that he was Odin's guest and under his protection. He taunted Thor further, pointing out that the Thunder God could not honorably attack him because he had left his own weapons at home in Jotunheim. However, he said, if Thor would go to Jotunheim he would consent to fight a duel. Thor readily agreed.

Hrungnir returned to Jotunheim, and word quickly spread that he was going to fight a duel with Thor. Hrungnir was by far the strongest of the giants, but Thor was one of the strongest of the Aesir, and easily the most dangerous. The giants worried about what to do.

Eventually they decided to create a second for Hrungnir: an immense clay man they called Mokkerkalfe (Mist-calf). He was nine *rasts* tall and three *rasts* broad across the chest. He had a horse's heart, which was the largest the giants could find, but even this trembled and fluttered when Thor approached, accompanied by his servant Thjalfi. Hrungnir's heart was made of stone like the rest of him, and he stood his ground. Mokkerkalfe, on the other hand, wet himself at the sight of Thor.

Thjalfi ran ahead to where Hrungnir stood, armed with a stone shield and an immense club of flint. He told the giant that it was foolish to hold his stone shield in front of him, because Thor intended to sink into the ground and attack him from below.

Hearing this, Hrungnir put his shield on the ground and stood on top of it, taking his stone club in both hands. A flash of lightning blinded Hrungnir temporarily, and when he regained his sight he could see Thor charging toward him.

The Thunder God threw his great hammer Mjolnir, and the giant threw his own club to intercept the hammer in mid-air. The collision broke Hrungnir's club in two; one part fell to

RASTS

A *rast* ("rest") was the distance one could walk between rest stops. It has been estimated as a little over 7 miles. This makes the clay man Mokkerkalfe over 63 miles tall and 21 miles wide. Exaggeration was a common feature of Viking tales, and we can assume that the size of the clay giant has grown in the telling.

(Opposite) Thor's hammer Mjolnir breaks Hrungnir's stone club and strikes the giant's head. (Ivy Close Images / Alamy)

the ground and the other struck Thor in the head, knocking him down. Having broken Hrungnir's club, Mjolnir struck the giant's head, killing him instantly.

The giant toppled over like an immense felled tree. One of his feet came to rest across Thor's body, and even with his divine strength the Thunder God was unable to move the foot off him. Meanwhile Thjalfi attacked Mokkerkalfe, who fell with little honor.

Thor was still trapped under Hrungnir's foot. Thjalfi tried to help lift it off him, but it was too heavy. The other Aesir also tried, but no one was able to lift the giant's foot and free Thor. At last, Thor's three-day-old son Magni ("Strong") arrived. His mother was the giantess Jarnsaxa ("Iron-knife") and only he had the strength to lift Hrungnir's foot and free his father.

The flint from Hrungnir's weapon was still stuck in Thor's head. He consulted a wise-woman named Groa to remove it, but while she was singing her magic songs Thor started telling her the stories of his adventures (see *The Stone in Thor's Head*). She forgot her singing, and the stone remained lodged in Thor's head forever after.

Thrym's Wedding

This semi-comic tale from the *Thrymskvida* puts Thor in an undignified position when his famous hammer is stolen and he must adopt a disguise to get it back. Like his adventures in Utgard, the story makes Thor as much a figure of fun as a hero. The story of how Thrym was able to steal Thor's hammer is either missing or not told.

Thrym tries to kiss Thor. W. G. Collingwood, 1908. (PD-US)

After finding his hammer missing, Thor went to Loki and demanded that he help find it. Loki borrowed Freyja's feathered garment, which allowed him to take the shape of a falcon, and eventually discovered that the culprit was Thrym ("Uproar"), the king of the giants of Jotunheim.

Thrym admitted that he had Mjolnir, but he told Loki that it was hidden eight *rasts* (about 56 miles) beneath the earth. He said that the Aesir would never get it back until they gave him the goddess Freyja as his wife.

Thor drops his bridal disguise and prepares to slaughter Thrym and his kin in this Swedish illustration from 1865. (PD-US)

When Loki took this news back to Asgard, Freyja was horrified. Her rage made the halls of Asgard shake and shattered her famous necklace Brisingamen. She wanted nothing to do with Thrym, and the Aesir were forced to come up with another plan.

Heimdall was the guardian of the rainbow bridge Bifrost that connected Asgard to the mortal realm of Midgard ("middle-earth"). He was among the wisest of the Aesir and had the gift of foresight. He suggested a plan that would win Mjolnir back and give Thor his revenge against the thief.

Heimdall suggested that the Aesir should disguise Thor as Freyja, dressing him in bridal garments and fastening the repaired Brisingamen around his neck. Accompanied by Loki dressed as a bridesmaid, the two would go to Jotunheim and reclaim Mjolnir when Thrym brought it out for the wedding ceremony.

Humiliated by the thought of dressing as a bride, Thor was as reluctant to take part in Thrym's wedding as Freyja had been. Loki was finally able to overcome Thor's reluctance by pointing out that unless the Aesir recovered his hammer quickly, the giants would be able to walk into Asgard and take over. Hearing this, Thor grudgingly agreed to the plan.

Dressed as a bride and bridesmaid, Thor and Loki set out for Jotunheim in Thor's magical chariot. Thrym was taken in by the deception, although he was surprised when his "bride" devoured a whole ox and eight salmon at the wedding feast, as well as drinking three *salds* (about 66 gallons) of mead. Loki quickly explained that Freyja had been so excited about her impending marriage that she had not eaten for eight days and nights before setting out for Jotunheim.

Later in the feast, Thrym leaned across and tried to kiss his "bride," but the sight of Thor's burning eyes glaring out from beneath the bridal veil made him change his mind. Once again, Loki saved the situation, explaining that as well as being unable to eat, Freyja had not slept for eight nights as she longed for her wedding day.

At last Thrym ordered his servants to bring Mjolnir into the hall so it could consecrate his wedding. As soon as the hammer was laid in the lap of the "bride" Thor leaped up and smashed Thrym's skull with it, and then slaughtered all the wedding guests. With Mjolnir recovered and the threat from Jotunheim averted, Thor and Loki returned to Asgard.

Thor and Geirrod

The earliest source for this story is the *Thorsdrapa* of Eilifr Godrunarson. Another version is told by Snorri Sturluson in the *Skaldskaparmal*, but there are significant differences between the two. Thor's servant Thjalfi plays a major role in the *Thorsdrapa* but Snorri omits him from his version entirely, except where he quotes the *Thorsdrapa* extensively at the end of his telling of the tale.

Loki's Promise

It happened that Loki was flying about in Freyja's falcon form and came to Geirrodsgard, the home of the giant Geirrod. Loki flew down to Geirrod's hall and peered in through a window, but Geirrod spotted the bird and ordered one of his servants to bring it to him. Loki amused himself for some time evading the servant's attempts to capture him, but at last the servant caught hold of his feet and he was unable to get away.

Geirrod suspected that this was no ordinary bird. He questioned Loki, but he did not answer. Geirrod locked Loki in a chest and starved him for three months before he was ready to speak. To save his own life, Loki promised Geirrod that he would bring Thor to his hall without his hammer or his belt of strength. Without these magical gifts, Thor would be at a great disadvantage. Geirrod agreed and let Loki go.

THE STONE IN THOR'S HEAD

In *Lapponia,* a 17th-century account of the Lapps of northern Scandinavia, German scholar Johann Scheffer observed that the Lapps kept a rough wooden image of the Thunder God:

> Into his head they drive a nail of iron or steel, and a small piece of flint to strike
> fire with, if he hath a mind to it.

Through his association with lightning Thor was also regarded as a fire god in some ways, and the legend of how a piece of flint became lodged in Thor's head may reflect a Viking age practice of using an idol of Thor to make a ritual fire.

Thor's Journey

Returning to Asgard, Loki talked Thor into mounting another expedition against the giants. Giant-slaying was one of Thor's favorite pastimes, so this was not a difficult task. However, the available sources do not tell how Loki persuaded the Thunder God to leave his hammer and magical belt behind. This must have been a great feat even for silver-tongued Loki, but it goes unrecorded.

Accompanied by his servant Thjalfi, Thor set out for Jotunheim. Along the way, he visited a giantess whose name was Gridr ("Greed"). She was the mother of Vidar, the Aesir god of vengeance, whose father was Odin.

Gridr warned Thor that Geirrod was a cunning and dangerous giant. Seeing that he was not carrying his magical gear, she lent him her own belt of strength, a pair of iron gloves, and a magical staff named Gridarvolr.

Leaving Gridr's house, Thor traveled to the banks of the River Vimer, which was the largest of all rivers. Buckling on his borrowed belt of strength, he braced himself with the staff Gridarvolr and waded into the rushing water. The waters rose and rose until they almost covered his shoulders, and Thor spoke a verse (possibly a magic spell):

Wax not, Vimer,
Since I intend to wade
To the gards (lands) of giants.
Know, if you wax,
Then waxes my asa (Aesir, divine) might
As high as the heavens.

Translation by Rasmus B. Anderson, 1901

Looking up, Thor saw Geirrod's daughter Gjalp standing astride the stream and, as Snorri delicately puts it, "causing its growth." He drove her off by throwing a huge stone at her, and was able to reach out and grab a shrub to pull himself out of the river.

Thor pulls himself from the River Vimer. Lorenze Frolich, 1906. (PD-US)

Geirrod's Hall

When Thor and Thjalfi arrived at Geirrod's hall, the giant showed them to a guest room that was furnished with a single chair. Thor sat down, but quickly became aware that the chair was rising toward the ceiling. Bracing the staff Gridarvolr against the rafters, he pushed himself down against the seat.

He heard a great crash, accompanied by agonized screaming. Geirrod's two daughters, Gjalp and her sister Greip, had hidden under the chair and were lifting it up to crush their visitor against the ceiling; when Thor pushed himself down, he broke their backs.

Thor went into Geirrod's hall, where fires were burning all along the walls. Geirrod reached into one of the fires with a pair of tongs and pulled out a red-hot iron wedge, which he hurled at the Thunder God. When Thor caught the missile in his borrowed iron gloves, Geirrod ducked behind an iron pillar, but Thor threw the red-hot wedge so hard that it passed right through the pillar, through Geirrod's body, through the wall, and into the ground outside.

With Geirrod dead, Thor and Thjalfi fought their way out of his hall, slaughtering countless giants as they escaped.

THOR AND HARBARD

This tale is told in the *Harbardsljod* ("Lay of Harbard") in the *Poetic Edda*. The dialogue form of the original telling is preserved here.

Harbard ("Hoary-beard") is one of many names by which Odin is referred to in Old Norse poetry. It may be that he is playing a trick on Thor by disguising himself as an argumentative old ferryman, or it may be that this Harbard is nothing more than he appears to be. In either case, the *flyting* contest gives Thor ample scope to brag of his many achievements.

This poem makes reference to many other myths, some of which can be found in this book. Explanatory notes, when needed, are given in italics between the lines of dialogue.

Harbard's Ferry

Returning to Asgard after one of his expeditions into Jotunheim, Thor arrived at the shores of a sound and saw an old ferryman with his boat standing on the other side. Demanding passage across the water, he was refused in the most insulting terms.

Thor: Who is that knave standing by the sound?

Harbard: Who is that churl shouting across the water?

Thor: Ferry me across the sound and tomorrow I'll tell you. I have a basket on my back with the best of food inside. Before I set out I filled up on herring and oats.

Harbard: You're so full of how great your breakfast was, so you mustn't know. You'll have a sorry homecoming. I hear your mother is dead.

Thor: You're giving me the worst news anyone can hear when you say my mother is dead.

Thor's mother is reported by various sources to have been the goddess Frigga or a giantess named Fjorgyn or Erda. There is nothing in this myth or any other to suggest that Harbard is telling the truth here; this seems to be some kind of insult, perhaps comparable to the "yo' mama" snaps of more recent times.

Harbard: You don't look like someone who owns three country dwellings, standing there bare-legged and in rags like a beggar. You don't even have any breeches.

According to myth, Thor owned three homes. Bilskirnir ("Lightning-crack") in Asgard boasted 540 floors and was the largest building ever constructed. It was there that Thor lived with Sif and their children. Thrudheim ("World of Strength") and

(Opposite) Harbard and Thor's *flyting* contest. Thor asks the ferryman Harbard (who may be Odin in disguise) for a ride, but receives only insults.

41

Thor and Harbard face off in this pair of book illustrations. W. G. Collingwood, 1908. (PD-US)

Thrudvang ("Field of Power") seem to have been country estates outside Asgard. Since Thor has not yet revealed his name, either Harbard has already recognized him (strengthening the possibility that he is Odin in disguise) or this line is out of order.

Thor: Bring your boat over here and I'll tell you where to land. And tell me, who owns the boat?

Harbard: Hildolf is his name. I'm looking after it for him. He lives in Radso Sound, and he's no fool. He told me not to carry robbers or horse thieves – only good men, and only men I know. So tell me your name if you want a ride across.

Hildolf ("War Wolf") was another son of Odin, but little else is known about him. This may be another clue that Harbard is Odin in disguise.

Thor: I'll tell you my name, and the names of my kin too. I am Odin's son, Meili's brother, and Magni's father. You're talking to Thor himself. And who are you?

Harbard: I am called Harbard. I don't usually hide my name.

Thor: And why should you, unless you're a criminal?

Harbard: I might have committed a crime or two, but I can defend myself against your sort unless I'm fated to die here.

Thor: It seems too much bother to wade across the strait to you and get my clothes wet – but I'll pay you back for your insults if you make me come over there, little man!

Harbard: I'll stand right here and wait for you. You haven't faced a stouter foe since Hrungnir's death.

Thor: I remember Hrungnir. He was a brave giant with a head of solid rock. Still I dropped him, and saw him fall. What have you done, Harbard?

Harbard: I spent five winters with Fiolvari on the isle of Algron. We fought and made slaughter, won through many perils, and enjoyed our pleasures.

This seems to be the only reference to Fiolvari and the island of Algron. It might be supposed that this line refers to a now-lost reference to one of Odin's exploits.

Thor: How did the women like you, then?

Harbard: They were spirited, and not meek; clever, and not kind. They twisted a rope out of sand and dug the earth out of a deep valley. I was the

Popular from the 5th century to the 16th, *flyting* was a bloodless duel that took the form of an exchange of insults, often in verse. The name comes from the Old Norse *flyta,* meaning provocation. Sometimes *flyting* contests ended in a clear victory, and at other times they formed a prelude to physical combat between two heroes. When Loki insulted the Aesir at Aegir's feast, his abuse took the form of *flyting* against all of them in turn.

only one more cunning than they were. I lay with the seven sisters and shared their love and pleasures. What did you do, Thor?

Thor: I killed Thjazi, the terrible giant, and threw his eyes up into the heavens where they shine like stars. They are proof of the greatest of my deeds. What have you done, Harbard?

The giant Thjazi, son of Allvaldi, once kidnapped the goddess Idun, the holder of the magical apples that kept the Aesir from aging. After he was killed, his eyes were cast up into the heavens to become stars. According to one source, it was Odin who did this; another source credits Loki with the deed. This is the only source where Thor claims credit.

Harbard: I used great seductive arts against the riders of the night when I enticed them from their husbands. Hlebard gave me a magic wand, but I charmed his wits from him.

Hlebard is a dwarf who made a magic wand for Odin. He also fashioned the arrow with which a jealous Loki tricked the blind god Hod into killing Balder, the fairest of the Aesir. The words "the riders of the night" are thought by some scholars to refer to giantesses and witches in general.

Thor: Then you repaid good gifts with bad ones.

Harbard: One tree gets the scrapings from another: each one looks out for itself. What have you done, Thor?

Thor: I was in the east, and slew the cunning and evil Jotun brides as they went to the mountain. The Jotun race would have been great if they had all lived, but now there's not one of them left in Midgard. What have you done, Harbard?

Thor is bragging of his numerous giant-slaying exploits.

Harbard: I was in Valland, devoted to warfare. I stirred up the princes, and never reconciled them. Odin has all the nobles that fall in battle; Thor only has the thralls.

Valland ("Land of the Foreigners") is an Old Norse term for southern and western Europe, which was occupied by Celtic and Roman-descended peoples. Thralls were the lowest class of Norse society, comparable to the serfs of the Middle Ages. Harbard is bragging of stirring up war in Valland (another hint that he may in fact be Odin), and insults Thor by saying that only the lowest come to his halls after falling in battle.

Thor: You would divide folk unequally among the Aesir, if you only had the power.

This 17th-century manuscript illustrates the legend that the River Van (unknown today) flows from the jaws of the bound Fenrir. (PD-US)

Harbard: Thor has too much strength and not enough courage. Fear drove you to hide in a glove and hardly remembered you were Thor. You didn't even dare sneeze or cough in case Fialar might hear you.

This is a reference to Thor's humiliating misadventures with Utgardaloki. Fialar is the name of a cockerel that was prophesied to crow at the onset of Ragnarok; Harbard seems to be saying that Thor was so frightened that he thought the world would end if he was heard.

Thor: Harbard, you wretch! I would strike you dead, if I could stretch my arm across the sound.

Harbard: Why would you stretch your arm across the sound when I have given you no offense? But what have you done, Thor?

Harbard was telling no more than the truth in his previous line, and so, although he has clearly insulted Thor, he has technically not slandered him.

Thor: I was in the east, and I defended a river against the sons of Svarang. They pelted me with stones, but enjoyed little success. They finally begged me for peace. What have you done, Harbard?

There is no other mention of the "sons of Svarang" in any surviving source. Thor says he was in the east, which generally refers to Jotunheim, so this may be a reference to a lost giant-slaying adventure. It is worth noting that Thor fought his way from a river during his journey to the home of the giant Geirrod, although it cannot be proved that this line refers to that adventure.

Harbard: I was in the east, and held converse with a certain lass. I dallied with that fair one, and we spent a long time together. I delighted that gold-bright one, and our games amused her.

Odin had liaisons with several giantesses, including Grid with whom he fathered Vidar. This may be a reference to her. Odin also boasts of his sexual conquests among the giantesses in the Havamal.

Thor: Then you had kind damsels there?

Harbard: I could have used your help in keeping that maid happy, Thor!

Thor: I would have given it to you, if I had had the chance.

Harbard: I would have trusted you if you hadn't betrayed my confidence.

The meaning of this line is obscure. It may be a reference to the prophecy of Ragnarok, which tells that the wolf Fenrir will slay Odin after Thor refuses to fight it. Loki also throws this in Thor's face during Aegir's feast.

Thor: I am not such a heel-chafer as an old leather shoe in spring.

Harbard: What have you done, Thor?

Thor: I cudgeled the berserkers' brides on Hlesey. They had committed the worst of crimes, and seduced the whole people.

Hlesey is the Danish island of Læso. The name translates as "Hler's island"; Hler is another name for Aegir. Aegir had nine daughters with the sea-goddess Ran, each named after a type of wave; however, it is not clear whether there is any connection between them and the women mentioned in this line.

Harbard: That was a dastardly act, Thor, to cudgel women.

Thor: They were she-wolves, and scarcely women. They crushed my ship, which I had secured with props, threatened me with iron clubs, and drove Thjalfi away. What have you done, Harbard?

Harbard: I was in the army that was sent out to raise war-banners and redden spears.

Thor: Tell of that now, since you went out to offer us hard terms.

Harbard: That shall be secured by a hand ring such as judges use, who wish to reconcile us.

Multiple sources tell us that the temples of Thor contained sacred gold rings upon which the Vikings were accustomed to swearing their most sacred and binding oaths. When Alfred the Great negotiated a peace with the Danish king Guthrum in 876, the Danes swore their peace oaths on a "holy ring" associated with the worship of Thor.

Thor: Where did you learn such words? I never heard anything so irritating!

Harbard: I learned them from men – ancient men, whose home is in the woods.

Thor: You certainly give a good name to grave-mounds, when you call them homes in the woods.

Harbard: That is how I speak of such a subject.

Thor: You will regret your clever words if I decide to ford the sound. Louder than a wolf you'll howl, I swear, if you get a touch of my hammer.

Harbard: Sif has a gallant at home. You'll be anxious to find him. You'd do better to pursue that task instead.

This line appears to be nothing more than an insult. There is nothing in the surviving sources to suggest that Sif carried on any affairs while she was married to Thor, although she did give birth to the winter-god Ullr by an unnamed father. Thor is sometimes named as "Ullr's foster-father." At Aegir's feast Loki also accuses Sif of infidelity, claiming to have been intimate with her himself – but Loki is well known as a liar and slanderer, and his word cannot be taken at face value.

Thor: You say whatever comes to mind as long as it will annoy me, you low-minded scoundrel! I believe you are lying.

Harbard: I believe I am telling the truth. You are traveling slowly; you would have arrived long since if you had assumed another form.

Thor: Harbard, you wretch! Rather is it you who have held me up.

Harbard: I would never have thought that a ferryman could delay the travels of the great Aesir Thor.

Thor: I will give you one piece of advice: row your boat over here. Let us cease from threats; approach the sire of Magni.

Harbard: Go away from the sound. Passage across is refused you.

Thor: Show me the way, then, if you won't ferry me across the water.

Harbard: That's too little to refuse. It's a long way: an hour to the stock, another hour to the stone. Then keep to the left-hand way until you reach Verland. There Fiorgyn will find her son Thor and show him his kinsmen's ways to Odin's land.

Verland is "the land of men" according to some scholars, making it another name for Midgard. Since Thor is on his way back from "the east" he may not have left Jotunheim by the time he reaches Harbard's ferry.

Thor: Can I get there today?

Harbard: With some effort you may get there while the sun is up.

Thor: Our talk shall now be short, since you only answer me with mockery. If we meet again, I'll pay you back for refusing to ferry me.

Harbard: Just go to where all the powers of evil may have you.

The poem ends abruptly at this point. We are left to suppose that Thor was forced to walk around the inlet since Harbard refused to ferry him across.

FENRIR

Fenrir ("Fen-dweller") is a monstrous wolf that is generally accepted to have been the offspring of Loki and a giantess named Angrboda ("Grief-bringer") along with Jormungand the Midgard Serpent and Hel, the goddess who ruled a dark realm of the dead that bore her name. A reference in the *Voluspa* might be interpreted as contradicting this, however: it implies that Fenrir was raised by a witch. It also states that the great wolf that devoured the moon was one of Fenrir's offspring.

Fenrir was raised among the gods, growing quickly and reaching a prodigious size. Only the law-god Tyr dared go and feed him. When it was prophesied that Fenrir would be the doom of the Aesir, they decided to bind him with a great chain called *Laeding*. Fenrir snapped this immediately. A second chain was brought, named *Dromi*. This took Fenrir some effort to break, but he did so.

The Aesir turned to the dwarves, who fashioned a silken bond named *Gleipnir* out of such impossible things as the footfall of a cat and the breath of a fish. Distrustful, Fenrir refused to let the Aesir place it on him until Tyr agreed to place his hand in the wolf's mouth as a sign of good faith. *Gleipnir* was fastened, and when Fenrir found he could not escape, he bit off Tyr's hand.

At this signal the other Æsir threw the chain round the monster's neck.

Thor (on the left) helps bind the wolf Fenrir in this 1930s book illustration by Charles Edmund Brock. (The Bridgeman Art Library)

Although Tyr lost his hand, the wolf was bound and left chained to a rock until Ragnarok came.

RAGNAROK

Norse mythology is unlike the mythologies of most other cultures in that it contains a detailed description of the end of the world, in which even the gods are killed.

There are two main sources for the events of Ragnarok. The *Poetic Edda* contains a poem called *Voluspa*, in which a *volva* or seeress gives Odin a detailed prophecy about the end of the world. In *Gylfaginning*, in the *Prose Edda*, another account is given as part of a general account of the world and the gods: this quotes extensively from the *Voluspa*.

Ragnarok is mentioned in several other places in the *Eddas*, but only in passing. Usually a character taunts one of the gods with something from the prophecy, as when Loki taunts Thor with the fact that he will not save Odin from the wolf Fenrir.

The Old Norse word "Ragnarok" can be translated as "the fate of the gods." In one place in the *Lokasenna* a slightly different word form is used, which may be an accidental misspelling or a deliberate variation: *ragnarøkkr* instead of *ragnarok*. The translation of *ragnarøkkr* is "twilight of the gods," and it was taken by Richard Wagner as the title of the fourth opera in his Ring Cycle, *Gotterdämmerung*.

Fimbulwinter

Ragnarok will begin with Fimbulvetr ("the great winter," Fimbulwinter), a harsh and stormy winter that lasts for three years with no intervening summers. During this time, war and discord spread across the whole world. Family loyalty and other social ties break down completely as brothers kill their brothers for material gain:

> There are axe-ages, sword-ages,
> Shields are cleft in twain,
> There are wind-ages, wolf-ages,
> Ere the world falls dead.
>
> The Voluspa

Fimbulwinter will destroy all life in Midgard, except for a woman named Lif and a man named Lifthrasir ("Life" and "Lover of Life") who survive by hiding in a deep forest called Hoddmimis Holt. The location of this forest is unclear. Its name translates as "Hoard-Mimir's Wood." Mimir was a god of great wisdom who lost his head during a war between the Aesir and the Vanir. Odin consults Mimir's severed head for advice in this myth and others.

(Opposite) According to prophecy, Thor and the Midgard Serpent will kill each other at Ragnarok.

49

The Breaking of the Heavens

At the end of Fimbulwinter, a number of prodigious events take place. A great wolf swallows the sun, and another the moon. The stars are hurled down from the heavens. The earth is wracked by violent earthquakes that uproot trees and tumble mountains.

The wolf Fenrir breaks loose from the bonds in which he was placed by the Aesir. The Midgard Serpent stirs, thrashing in the sea and causing great waves to cover the land. Upon this flood comes Naglfari ("the ship of nails"), which is made from the nails of dead men. In some sources Loki stands at the tiller; in others, it is a giant named Hrym ("the decrepit"). The ship carries a horde of enemies who are not named, although Loki is said later to be leading the hordes of Hel and Thrym the Hrimthursar, or Frost Giants of Niflheim.

The Attack on Asgard

Fenrir and the Midgard Serpent advance side by side toward Bifrost, the rainbow bridge that connects

Surtur with his flaming sword. John Charles Dollman, 1909. (PD-US)

the mortal realm of Midgard with the Aesir's home of Asgard. Fenrir gapes so wide that his jaws span heaven and earth, and fire shoots from his eyes and nostrils. The Midgard Serpent vomits a flood of venom that covers the land and fouls the air. They cause such devastation that the heavens are torn in two.

Through the breach created by Fenrir and Jormungand come the Fire Giants of Muspelheim, led by their king Surtur. Wreathed in fire and wielding a sword brighter than the sun, Surtur destroys the rainbow bridge as his forces ride over it.

Heimdall, the god who watches over the rainbow bridge, sounds the horn Gjallarhorn to raise the alarm. Odin rides to Mimir's Well to consult the oracular head before returning to lead the Aesir into battle. The world-tree Yggdrasil begins to shake, and fear spreads throughout all creation. The final battle is about to be joined.

The Final Battle

The enemies of Asgard assemble on the field of Vigridr ("Surge of Battle"), which is one hundred *rasts* (almost 702 miles) on each side. Their forces are named as follows:

The wolf Fenrir and the Midgard Serpent Jormungand;

The Fire Giants, commanded by Surtur;

The hordes of Hel, commanded by Loki;

The Frost Giants, commanded by Thrym.

Against them are ranged the Aesir and the *einherjar*, those warriors who were chosen by the Valkyries and brought from the battlefield to Odin's hall at Valhalla, where they have spent the ages fighting all day and feasting all night.

The final battle is described as a series of individual combats, in which the gods fall one by one.

Odin, clad in bright mail and wielding his magical spear Gungnir, fights the wolf Fenrir. Thor stands beside him, but is locked in battle with the Midgard Serpent and unable to prevent Fenrir from slaying Odin.

Frey, the god of peace and fertility, faces the Fire Giant king Surtur, and is overcome after a fierce battle. It is said that Frey might have defeated Surtur if he had had his magical sword, which is capable of fighting on its own. However, he had lent it to his servant Skirnir, and falls before Surtur's fiery blade.

One-handed Tyr battles Garm, the monstrous dog that guarded the entrance to Hel, and they are both killed in the conflict.

After a hard struggle, Thor succeeds in killing the Midgard Serpent. However, he has little time to enjoy his victory. Overcome by the floods of venom that the dying Jormungand vomits forth, Thor staggers back nine paces and falls dead.

Meanwhile, Fenrir has swallowed Odin. Vidar, Odin's son by the giantess Gridr, steps forward and pries the wolf's jaws apart, tearing him to pieces (or, according to the *Voluspa*, stabbing him in the heart). Heimdall fights with Loki, and they kill each other.

As Fenrir, Loki, and Heimdall fall, Surtur flings fire over the earth, and the whole universe is consumed in the conflagration.

Thor fights the Midgard Serpent at Ragnarok. Book illustration by Charles Edmund Brock, 1930. (The Bridgeman Art Library)

Thor went forth against Jörmungand.

The New Age

After the flames subside, a new world, pleasant and fertile, will rise from the sea. Six gods are named as surviving Ragnarok: Vidar and his brother Vali, Thor's sons Modi and Magni, and the two dead gods Balder and Hod, who are released from Hel in this new age. They dwell peacefully in the plain of Ida, where Asgard formerly stood.

Lif and Lifthrasir emerge from the forest and feed on the morning dew. Their descendants will spread across the earth. A daughter of the sun, more beautiful than her mother, will take her place in the sky and bring light to the world.

It appears that these few are not alone in this new world. The righteous dwell in Gimle, where good and plentiful drink awaits them in the hall of Brimer. Snorri equates this with the Christian heaven. Another hall, made of red gold and called Sindre, stands on the Nida Mountains to the north, in what used to be the cold and gloomy realm of Niflheim.

However, all is not peace and plenty in this new world. The terrible hall of Nastrond (shores of the dead) is the abode of perjurers, adulterers and murderers. Its doors face north, letting in a bitter wind. Its walls are woven of living snakes that continually belch forth venom and those inside are forced to wade through streams of the poison.

Hvergelmir ("bubbling, boiling spring") is said to be even worse. Set in the former realm of Hel, it is inhabited by the terrible dragon Nidhogg, who sucks on the corpses of the dead.

The Midgard Serpent spews forth a flood of venom, poisoning Thor as he kills it. (Mary Evans Picture Library)

OTHER LEGENDS

The previous chapters have covered the major legends in which Thor appears, but there are others. For the most part they are shorter, and some consist only of passing mentions of his name and his deeds. They are gathered together in this chapter for the sake of completeness.

The Birth of Sleipnir

Thor plays a peripheral role in the legend that tells how Odin got his magical eight-legged steed Sleipnir, which is told in the *Gylfaginning*.

When the gods were first building Asgard, a builder came to them and offered to build a wall that would keep the realm safe from the giants. As his payment he demanded Freyja, the beautiful goddess of love and fertility, plus the sun and the moon.

After some discussion the Aesir agreed to his terms, but only if he could complete the work within one winter: if any work remained undone on the first day of the next summer, he would forfeit all payment. The unnamed builder replied that in order to complete the work in such a short time he would need the help of his horse Svadilfari ("unlucky traveler"), and at Loki's urging, the Aesir agreed.

Work started on the first day of winter, and Svadilfari hauled such immense quantities of stone that the Aesir began to worry. The work progressed rapidly, and with three days left until summer everything was complete except for the gateway. Faced with the prospect of losing Freyja and plunging the world into darkness by giving away the sun and the moon, the Aesir met to discuss their options.

At first they looked for someone to blame. It was decided that since the trickster Loki was well known for giving bad advice – he had, after all, urged the Aesir to agree to the builder's horse – the situation must be his fault. Threatened with a painful death if the building work was completed on time, Loki promised to make sure the Aesir were not compelled to make good on their bargain.

Turning himself into a mare, Loki distracted Svadilfari from his work and the two ran off together into the woods. The builder chased after them, wasting a great deal of time, but was unable to recover his horse. To make up the lost time, the builder grew to an enormous height. He was no ordinary man, but a giant in disguise. He had only felt safe coming to Asgard because Thor was away on one of his giant-slaying expeditions to the east.

(Overleaf) At a feast in Aegir's hall, Loki insults all the gods in turn. He only leaves when Thor threatens him. (See p. 29)

Loki (in the background) distracts the mighty horse Svadilfari. Dorothy Hardy, 1909. (PD-US)

Using his giant strength, the builder resumed work, determined to finish on time and win the goddess and the two lights of the sky. However, when the Aesir saw the giant's true nature they decided to disregard their agreement with him. They called upon Thor, who came back to Asgard right away and shattered the giant's skull with his hammer.

It was from Loki's dalliance with Svadilfari while in mare form that Odin's horse Sleipnir was conceived.

The Death of Balder

Odin's second son Balder was the most beautiful of the Aesir, and dearly loved by his mother Frigga. When both were troubled by prophetic dreams of his death, Frigga went to everything in the world and made each thing swear never to harm her son. However, she overlooked mistletoe: according to different sources, it was either too harmless or it was too young to take the oath.

Discovering this, the jealous Loki had a dwarf named Hlebard fashion an arrow (or a spear in some sources) of mistletoe. When Balder was showing off his newfound invulnerability by having the gods take turns trying to kill him, Loki gave the mistletoe weapon to the blind god Hod. Balder was killed.

Balder's funeral. W. G. Collingwood, 1908. (PD-US)

Thor appears only in the scene describing Balder's funeral. He blessed the funeral pyre with his hammer Mjolnir. Then, finding a dwarf named Litr was running around his feet, he kicked him into the flames where he was burnt alive. Nothing else is known about Litr; it seems that Thor kicked him purely out of annoyance.

The Binding of Loki

Eventually the Aesir became tired of Loki and his tricks. Seeing this, Loki fled to the mountains, where he built a house with four doors so that he could see anyone who approached from any direction. In the daytime he would often turn himself into a salmon and hide under a waterfall named Franangursfors, where he spent his time in divination and planning to evade whatever snares the Aesir might set for him.

Loki was making a fishing net when he saw the Aesir approaching his house. Before fleeing to the waterfall he threw it into the fire, but the wise god Kvasir saw the pattern of the net among the embers and directed the Aesir to make another. This is how fishing nets were invented. The Aesir threw the net into the water, with Thor holding one end and the rest of the gods holding the other, and dragged it downstream.

Loki hid between two stones in his salmon form, and the net passed over him. However, Odin sensed that the net had touched some living being, and the Aesir cast it again. This time, they weighted the bottom of the net so it touched the stream bed at every point, and Loki could not escape.

Loki leaped over the net and swam back to the waterfall. The Aesir split into two groups, one at either end of the net, while Thor waded behind it. When Loki leaped the net a second time, Thor caught him and barely managed to hold onto his slippery salmon form. Loki would have escaped if Thor had not caught him by the tail, and this is why all salmon have had slender tails ever since.

Loki was bound to a rock using the entrails of his son Nari, which the Aesir magically transformed into iron. Over his face they hung a snake, which continually dripped venom down upon him. He has been there ever since, and will be there until he breaks free at the start of Ragnarok. Loki's wife Siguna catches the snake's venom in a cup, but when she leaves to empty the cup the venom drips onto Loki's unprotected face, causing him such agony that his writhing produces earthquakes.

A 10th-century cross from Gosforth in England bearing an image of the bound Loki. (PD-US)

The Stone in Thor's Head

During his duel with the giant Hrungnir (see p. 33), Thor was struck by a piece of flint that lodged in his head. When he returned to his home at Thrudvang, he was visited by a wise woman named Groa, who offered to remove it for him.

Groa sang magic songs over Thor until the stone started to become loose. Thor was so happy, expecting that the stone would be out of his head in a moment, that he rewarded Groa by telling her of an adventure he had had with her husband, a hero named Orvandel the Bold.

The *Skaldskaparmal* does not retell the adventure in any detail, but it implies that Orvandel once accompanied the Thunder God on one of his giant-killing expeditions to Jotunheim. Thor carried Orvandel back in a basket, but one of his toes was sticking out and became frozen. Thor broke off the frozen toe and threw it into the sky, where it became a star that was still known as Orvandel's Toe.

Thor would have done better to wait until the stone was completely out of his head before telling his tale: Groa was so enchanted by this news of her husband (whom, Thor assured her, would be returning home before long) that she forgot to finish her magic song, and the flint remains embedded in Thor's head to this day.

For this reason, it is said to be unlucky to throw a piece of flint across the floor, for it causes the flint in Thor's head to shift.

Thor and the Dwarf Alvis

This story, told in the *Alvissmal,* is very different from the majority of Thor's adventures. His adversary is a cunning dwarf rather than a mighty giant, and Thor overcomes him by his wits rather than his strength.

The poem begins when the dwarf Alvis ("all-wise") comes to Thor and claims his daughter's hand in marriage, claiming that she was promised to him earlier. The story of how this promise came about appears to have been lost.

The girl's name is not mentioned in the poem, but Thor is only known to have had one daughter, a minor goddess named Thrud ("Strength"). The same name also belongs to one of the Valkyries, but it is not certain whether this is the same person as Thor's daughter.

Thor initially refuses since he was not at home when the match was made, and as the girl's father he should have been consulted. Alvis persists in his suit, though, boasting that he has traveled through all nine worlds and can answer any question Thor puts to him.

Thor proceeds to question the dwarf about the names of things: earth, heaven, the moon, the sun, the clouds, the wind, the calm, the sea, fire, the forest, the night, seed, and ale. Alvis responds to each question, giving not only the name by which mortals call each thing but adding the names used by the Aesir, the Vanir, the giants, the elves and the dwarves.

Thor questions Alvis in an early 20th-century illustration by W. G. Collingwood. (PD-US)

In the last stanza of the poem, Thor admits that he has never seen such wisdom as Alvis possesses. However, he says, the dwarf has been outwitted: it is dawn, and Alvis is above ground.

In some post-Viking folklore, members of certain nonhuman races – especially trolls – are turned to stone if the sun's rays strike them. Thor seems to be alluding to a similar weakness of the dwarves, although the poem ends abruptly without making this clear.

The Sayings of Grimnir

Thor does not appear in the *Grimnismal,* but Odin mentions him a few times in his conversation with the evil king Geirroth.

Thor's dwelling at Thrudheim is mentioned by name, and his mansion at Bilskirnir is described as having 540 floors, making it the greatest of all houses.

A few lines later, Odin names three rivers that Thor must wade on his way to the world-tree Yggdrasil where he will "sit as a judge" when "the Aesir-bridge" (Bifrost) burns: this presumably refers to the council of the Aesir after Heimdall sounds the alarm at Ragnarok. The rivers are named as Kormt and Örmt and "the Kerlaugs twain."

These rivers are also mentioned in *Gylfaginning* and *Skaldskaparmal,* where it is said that Thor always wades to the Aesir's meetings at Yggdrasil, preferring not to ride like the other gods.

(Opposite) Siguna protects the bound Loki. Arthur Rackham (PD-US)

THOR THE GOD

The surviving myths of Thor tell us little about his role in the religion of the pagan Vikings. This is because the surviving sources come from the Christian era and have been purged of religious content. However, there are some traces of Thor the god in the work of chroniclers who viewed the world of the Norsemen from the outside.

Earliest Traces

The worship of Thor goes back beyond Viking times. Although the Norse religion and its pantheon are best known for their role in Viking culture, they are a continuation of a Germanic religion first reported by Roman writers some 700 years before the first Viking raid struck England.

Donar (Germany)

In the first century CE, the Romans' conquest of Gaul brought them into contact with the Germanic peoples who lived east of the Rhine and north of the Danube. Around the year 98 the historian Tacitus published the *Germania*, an account of the Germanic peoples and their homelands.

In typical Roman fashion, Tacitus sought to describe the gods of the Germans by comparing them to Greco-Roman deities. He equated Odin with Mercury, Tyr with Mars, and Thor with Hercules, but he does not record their Germanic names. In classical myth, Hercules was famed for his strength and his weapon of choice was a huge club: the parallels to Thor's character and his iconic hammer are obvious.

Twenty years or so later, in the *Annals*, Tacitus again refers to a cult of "Hercules" among the Germanic peoples, mentioning a wood that was sacred to him.

It is from later sources that we learn the Germanic name of this deity. A brooch found in Bavaria bears the runic inscription *Donar*. The brooch dates to the 7th century, almost 200 years before the accepted start of the Viking period.

Thunor (England)

The pagan Anglo-Saxons established England ("Angle-Land") after the Roman Empire abandoned Britain in the 5th century CE. They brought their Germanic gods with them from their homelands, including a Thunder

God named Thunor. Place-names like Thundersley in Essex, Thundridge in Hertfordshire, and Thursley in Surrey are thought to be derived from his name. It is also found in Thursday, a day of the week traditionally associated with Thor (Torsdag in Danish, Norwegian, and Swedish; Donnerstag in German; Donderdag in Dutch). Hammer pendants have been found in Anglo-Saxon graves in eastern England, dating to the 6th century.

Documentary evidence for the worship of Thunor is scant. Like the Vikings, the Anglo-Saxons did not make much use of writing until they adopted Christianity. However, a 9th-century baptism vow from Old Saxony (now northern Germany) forsakes "Thunaer and Woden" as well as the Devil. The Church must have regarded these two pagan deities as a particular threat to single them out in this way.

Interestingly, an Old English text called *The Dialogue of Salomon and Saturnus* mentions Thunor striking the Devil with a fiery axe. As in post-Viking Scandinavia, it appears that Thor was partially rehabilitated as a hero after the Anglo-Saxons embraced Christianity.

Richard Doyle's *The God Thor Chasing the Dwarfs* (1878) shows Thor as a sky-god. The *Eddas* depict him somewhat differently. (Photo © The Maas Gallery, London / The Bridgeman Art Library)

The Viking Thor

Thor the god remains something of an enigma. Although there are plenty of stories about Thor's exploits dating from after the Viking Age, comparatively little is known about how he was worshiped in Viking times.

Temples and Sacred Groves

Archaeological traces of Norse temples are rare. There are written accounts of Christian missionaries destroying them, and it is thought that they built churches on the same sites, obscuring or destroying any traces of the pagan temples in the process. The few detailed written descriptions of Norse temples imply that Thor was usually worshiped in conjunction with other major deities, often Odin and Frey.

Sacred groves are reported by many Christian writers. The 11th-century German chronicler Adam of Bremen reports one at Old Uppsala, and the Irish king Brian Boru is said to have burned a grove in Dublin that was dedicated to Thor. The size of the grove may be judged from the fact that this task took a month.

Adam of Bremen described a temple at the Swedish capital of Gamla Uppsala (Old Uppsala) around 1070, late in the Viking Age. The temple was adorned with gold and had a golden chain hanging from the gables. Inside was an image of Thor (whom Adam described as "the mightiest"), flanked by images of Odin and Frey.

A 16th-century image of a pagan Norse temple, based in part on the writings of Adam of Bremen. The tree denotes the sacred grove, and the head at the right of the picture may be a sacrificial victim in a spring. (PD-US)

Human and animal sacrifices were hung on trees in a nearby grove. A spring in the grove was used for human sacrifice by drowning. "A living man is plunged into it," wrote Adam, "and if he does not reappear it is a sign that the people's wishes will be fulfilled."

Archaeological excavations at Gamla Uppsala have failed to find any trace of the temple and grove that Adam described. Excavations conducted in 1926 found the remains of an earlier structure beneath an 11th-century church on the site, but there was no conclusive proof that this was the temple described by Adam.

The *Eyrbyggja Saga* tells of a long feud between two Icelandic chieftains in the 10th and 11th centuries. It includes a rare Norse description of a pagan temple:

> It was a mighty building. There was a door in the side wall, nearer to one end of it; inside this door stood the posts of the high-seat, and in them were nails that were called the Divine Nails. The inside was a very sacred place. Right inside, at the far end, was a chamber, the same shape as a church chancel these days. In the middle of the floor was a stand like an altar, and on this lay an arm-ring, weighing twenty ounces, and all in one piece; men swore all their oaths on this. Also on the stand was the bowl for the blood of the sacrifice, and in it the blood-twig – like a holy-water sprinkler – which was used to sprinkle the blood of sacrificed beasts. And all around the stand the gods (i.e., idols) were set out in that holy place.

THUNDERSTONES

In Britain and Scandinavia, prehistoric stone axes found in the fields were commonly thought to be thunderbolts that had fallen to earth, splitting trees and damaging houses. A superstition once common in Europe held that one of these stones would protect a house from lightning if it were placed in the chimney, the roof, or under the threshold; the exact location varied according to local tradition.

A design on a Swedish runestone shows Thor's Hammer. The face at the top of the image may be of the god himself. (PD-US)

Idols

Idols of Thor and other gods are mentioned in several of the later sagas and histories, when Christian kings and missionaries destroy them.

Arabic accounts report that the Rus – Swedish Vikings who traveled east along Europe's great rivers – took idols on their journeys. These were wooden stakes with human-like faces, which could be set in the ground: the Rus prayed to them for success in their business dealings, repaying divine favors with animal sacrifices.

An image of Thor in a temple at Thrandheim, Norway, sat in a chariot drawn by two model goats; the whole construction was covered in gold and silver and mounted on wheels:

> Thor sat in the middle [i.e. between the temple's other idols]. He was the most highly honored. He was huge, and adorned with gold and silver. Thor sat in a chariot, and was very splendid. Two goats, very well-wrought, were harnessed in front of the chariot. The chariot and the goats ran on wheels. A rope of twined silver was around the goats' horns, and the whole thing was made with very fine craftsmanship.
>
> The Flateyarbok

Priests

Norse sources give various names for priests – *godi* and *gydja*, *vifill*, *lytir*, *thulr*, *thegn*, *volva* and *seidmadr* are known – but there seems to have been no professional priesthood. Instead, community leaders such as *jarls* also acted as religious leaders, and were described using one of these terms according to the nature of the religious activity in which they were involved at the time.

Rituals

Little is known about how Thor was actually worshiped. Various sagas and other literary sources make occasional mention of Vikings praying to Thor for good luck or good weather, and in 876 Danish leaders in England sealed a peace with King Alfred the Great by swearing on "holy rings" associated with the worship of Thor. These may be similar to the arm ring mentioned in the *Eyrbyggja Saga* above. Several runestones call upon Thor to protect a person or an area, or simply to witness the carving of the runes and the raising of the stone.

However, the sagas do not describe religious rituals in detail – perhaps because the details would have been very familiar to both the writers and their readers and needed no elaboration. Christian writers like Adam of Bremen focus on lurid descriptions of human and animal sacrifice, and say little about other forms of worship.

There were various festivals, or *blots*, throughout the year, but none was specifically dedicated to Thor: the Icelandic festival of Thorrablot seems to have been invented by university students in 1873.

Sacrifices

Adam of Bremen gives a detailed account of pagan sacrifices at Old Uppsala, which is very similar to Tacitus' accounts of German rituals from the *Germania*:

> If sickness or famine threaten they sacrifice to Thor; if war, to Odin, and if a wedding is to be celebrated they sacrifice to Frey. There is also a festival at Uppsala every nine years common to all the lands of Sweden. Attendance at this event is compulsory and it is the universal practice for kings and peoples and everyone to send offerings to Uppsala and – a cruel thing – those who have become Christians may secure exemption, but only on payment of a fine. The sacrifice consists of the slaughter of nine males whose bodies are hung in a grove near the temple, a sanctuary so holy that each tree is regarded as itself a deity, in consequence of the death and decay of the victims. Dogs and horses hang there beside human beings, and a Christian has told me that he has seen there as many as seventy-two carcasses hanging there side by side.

The Sign of the Hammer

Pendants in the form of Thor's magical hammer Mjolnir have been found across the Viking world. It seems to have been as popular among pagan Vikings as the cross was among Christians. At least one stone mold dating to the Viking Age has impressions of both a Christian cross and Thor's hammer, indicating that the Thor's hammer charm retained its popularity up to – and perhaps beyond – the time when the Vikings converted to Christianity.

A Thor's Hammer pendant from Mandemark, Møn, Denmark. (PD-US)

Another similarity between the cross and the hammer emerges from a series of references in historical and mythological sources. Pagan Vikings sometimes made a gesture indicating Thor's hammer as a sign of blessing or purification, in much the same way that Christians made, and still make, the sign of the cross.

The *Heimskringla* tells that Hakon the Good, an early Christian king of Norway, was bowed by pressure from his people into making winter sacrifices during a pagan festival at Hlader. When the drinking horn was passed to him, he made the sign of the cross over it to protect himself from the heathen nature of the proceedings. When eyebrows were raised one of his friends defended him, saying that he was actually making the sign of the hammer, as they were all accustomed to doing.

In the legends, too, Thor's hammer is shown to have the power to deliver blessings. In the *Thrymskvida*, Thor is forced to disguise himself as a bride to recover his stolen hammer, which he does when it is laid upon the "bride's" lap to sanctify the wedding. This suggests a similar practice to the Christian one of using crosses to confer blessings upon rituals and individuals.

The High-Seat Pillars

The Ondvegissulur, or high-seat pillars, stood either side of the master's seat in a Viking house. The folklorist H. R. Ellis Davidson suggests that they had a symbolic function linked to the sanctity of the great trees in a sacred grove, or the "lucky tree" that was sometimes planted beside a house to protect it.

It was apparently a common practice for settlers approaching Iceland to throw their high-seat pillars overboard and claim the land wherever they washed ashore. The *Landnamabok* tells of one follower of Thor named Thorolf Mostrarskegg ("most-beard") who packed up a shrine to the god and took it with him to Iceland. Approaching the coast, Thorolf threw the god's high-seat pillars (or perhaps, pillars carved with the likeness of Thor) into the sea instead of his own, letting the god decide where he would reside in this new land. The shrine was rebuilt next to the house, and is described in the *Eyrbyggja Saga*.

Thor and Christianity

The worship of the Norse gods – Thor in particular – died hard in the Viking lands. The Danish archaeologist Johannes Brondsted reported multiple stones on which the image of Thor's hammer appeared alongside that of the Christian cross, and images of Thor have been found on carved stone crosses in churchyards in northern England. Many Vikings saw no reason why they should not adopt the worship of "the White Christ" alongside their traditional faith. In the 12th century the Saxon churchman Aelnoth of Canterbury wrote:

> As long as things go well, the Swedes seem willing to acknowledge Christ and honor him, but only as a formality. When things go wrong – bad harvests, droughts, storms and bad weather, enemy attacks or fires – they persecute the religion that they pretend to honor with action as well as words.

One Gaukathori, according to the Icelandic *Landnamabok*, "was very mixed in his faith; he believed in Christ, but invoked Thor in matters of seafaring and dire necessity." Gaukathori himself is quoted as saying to King (later saint) Olaf II of Norway: "If I must believe in a god, it is no worse to believe in the White Christ than any other."

Several histories record the efforts of Olaf and various other rulers and churchmen in tearing down the temples of the old religion, including the great pagan temple at Old Uppsala. Christian commentators tried to reconcile the new and old beliefs: the resurrection of Balder was likened to that of Christ, since both marked the beginning of a new age.

There are a few indications that the followers of Thor struck back. Davidson reports that one Icelander told a Christian missionary that Thor had challenged Christ to single combat, while a Norwegian tale tells of Thor taking part in a tug-of-war with Christ's champion, King Olaf Tryggvason.

Thor in Folklore

Over time, though, Thor and the other Norse gods receded into folklore and fairytales. Jacob Grimm and other 19th-century collectors of folklore recorded that trolls were afraid of lightning, and some tales tell that Thor is still at large, chasing down giants and their kin.

Thor never stopped being a popular personal name, along with compounds like Torsten ("Thor's stone"), Torvald ("Thor's ruler"), Torbjorn ("Thor's bear"), Thordis ("Thor's goddess"), and Thora (a feminine form of Thor). Place-names throughout the former Viking world begin with Thor-, Tor-, and other elements indicating a connection with the Thunder God.

Thor is also linked to a number of landscape features in northern and western Europe. Here are a few examples, showing the extent of his influence on local folklore.

Thor's Stone, a house-sized outcrop of red sandstone near the Wirral in Cheshire, England, is surrounded by various local legends that make it everything from the site of a local assembly or *thing* to a pagan altar (the blood of the victims accounting for the stone's red color) to a fallen thunderbolt to Mjolnir itself.

Further south, at The Devil's Jumps near Churt in Surrey, a large boulder by three hills is said to have been thrown by Thor at the Devil, who was annoying him by jumping from one hill to another.

Donderberg ("Thunder Mountain") near Dieren in the Netherlands is a hill that carries a legend that Donar/Thor crashed his chariot there after being overcome by the Midgard Serpent's venom at Ragnarok. The crash created two deep lakes, and according to local tradition the hammer Mjolnir surfaced from the depths when the floodwaters receded.

(*Overleaf*) Fighting giants is Thor's favorite pastime. A *kenning* (poetic nickname) for him was "the giant-slayer."

Thor battles the Midgard Serpent in this hand-colored engraving of Ragnarok. (Charles Walker / Topfoto)

THOR'S LEGACY

The spread of Christianity did not spell the end for Thor. Translations and retellings of the myths from the *Eddas* appeared throughout the 16th, 17th, and 18th centuries, but it was in the 19th century that Norse mythology became more than a mere historical curiosity. The reasons were many: among them were rising Norwegian nationalism, archaeological discoveries in Scandinavia and Britain, and the first publication of a theory that Vikings had visited North America centuries before Columbus.

The 19th Century

Just as 19th-century Romantics in Britain looked to classical myths and the legends of King Arthur, German Romantics turned to the world of Norse myth to help establish a national identity. Thor was referenced in many 19th-century works, including poems, paintings, and sculptures.

Popular consciousness of Norse-Germanic lore even affected the science of the day. In 1828, Swedish chemist Jons Jakob Berzelius named a newly discovered radioactive element Thorium in the Thunder God's honor.

American poet Henry Wadsworth Longfellow, best known today as the author of the epic poem *The Song of Hiawatha*, was among the 19th-century writers and artists fascinated by Norse culture. His 1839 collection *Voices of the Night* included several poems translated from Danish, Anglo-Saxon, and German. In 1863 he published *Tales of a Wayside Inn*, a collection that included 22 Norse-inspired poems collected together under the title *The Musician's Tale: The Saga of King Olaf.* The titles of individual poems included "The Challenge of Thor," "The Wrath of Odin," and "Thangbrand the Priest."

In Europe, perhaps the best-known proponent of the Viking revival was the composer Richard Wagner. His four-opera work *The Ring of the Nibelung* (better known as the *Ring Cycle*), composed between 1848 and 1874, was based on the *Volsung Saga*, a Norse epic that tells of Odin's meddling in the affairs of the Volsung clan. It is best known today for its iconic theme "The Ride of the Valkyries."

GORDON WAIN 83

The 20ᵗʰ Century

Interest in Norse myth and religion continued to grow in the early 20ᵗʰ century, especially in Germany. Under the influence of writers like Guido von List and Karl Maria Wiligut, societies were founded to study and promote Nordic culture, religion and mysticism. One of the most influential was the Thule Society, founded in 1911. As a defeated Germany struggled for a sense of identity in the aftermath of World War I, the Thule Society attracted many founding members of what would become the National Socialist Party.

Thor and Hitler

Adolf Hitler chose the swastika as the symbol for his new party because of its alleged Germanic heritage. Although the design was used by many ancient cultures, most significantly for Hitler it represented Thor and his thunderbolts in Norse tradition.

In 1935, SS chief Heinrich Himmler met with a group of German intellectuals and founded the *Ahnenerbe*, a society for the study of ancient history whose stated goal was to prove that Nordic peoples had once conquered the world. This was part of a Nazi effort to legitimize the concept of an Aryan race and its alleged right to world dominance.

The question of whether senior members of the SS and other Nazis observed a form of Germanic-Norse paganism is a complex one. Nazi philosophy was influenced by the work of Guido von List and others, but in *Mein Kampf* and elsewhere Hitler stated his opposition to a return to the worship of Thor and Odin. While some holidays – especially the summer and winter solstices – were celebrated under their Germanic names, Nazi paganism seems to have been more prevalent in postwar fiction and conspiracy theory than in actual fact.

Modern Neopaganism

In the late 1960s and early 1970s, renewed interest in Norse paganism arose in Iceland and elsewhere, apparently from the same kind of spiritual curiosity that led British and American hippies to study eastern, Celtic, and Native American mysticism. The Asatru ("Aesir Faith") movement began in 1972, and similar groups sprang up in Scandinavia, the USA, Germany,

NEO-NAZISM

The swastika remains a popular symbol among neo-Nazis to the present day. It has been joined in recent decades by the Thor's hammer emblem. Both symbols have spread to other far-right and white supremacist groups. The name "Thor's Hammer" has also been adopted by a Polish black metal band that the Anti-Defamation League accuses of racism. Followers of Asatru and other Norse-Germanic neopagans oppose the use of Thor's hammer by racist and far-right groups, and these groups have no apparent interest in neo-nazism.

and elsewhere. Norse neopaganism continues to grow and spread. It is a recognized religion in several countries, meaning that its adherents have the power to conduct weddings, funerals, and other legally significant ceremonies. Most Norse neopagans worship Thor alongside Odin, Frey, and other Norse deities.

The Comic-Book Thor

In August 1962, Marvel Comics published *Journey into Mystery* #83, which introduced the world to Thor in his best-known comic-book incarnation. Both alone and as a member of the Avengers, Thor has appeared in Marvel comics in every decade since. He has also appeared in live action and animated TV series (including guest appearances in series headlined by other Marvel characters), as well as movies (most recently 2011's *Thor*, 2012's *The Avengers* and 2013's *Thor 2: The Dark World*) and video games.

Marvel's Thor was not the first comic-book interpretation of the Norse god. In 1940, the short-lived *Weird Comics* featured a storyline about a scientist who gained the powers of the Norse god after being struck by lightning. Thor also appeared in various European comics in the 1970s and played a role in Neil Gaiman's celebrated *Sandman* series (published by Marvel's archrival DC Comics) as well as in Gaiman's novel *American Gods* and Douglas Adams' *The Long Dark Tea-Time of the Soul*. However, it is the Marvel version of the Norse god that has had the most lasting effect on popular culture.

The Marvel Thor has blond hair instead of red, but otherwise he is very similar to the character portrayed in the *Eddas*. His hammer and his great physical strength are his main attributes, and he usually takes a direct, often violent approach to any problems he encounters.

Thor did not come alone from the *Eddas* to the comics. The trickster Loki is a regular foe, appearing in multiple comic storylines as well as all three of the Marvel films that feature Thor. Loki actually made his Marvel debut in 1949, 13 years before Thor.

The Midgard Serpent, the deadliest of Thor's foes, debuted in 1952, and has appeared as Thor's nemesis since 1966. Thor #272 (June 1978) wove an almost direct retelling of Thor's adventures against Utgardaloki into the Marvel continuity. The following month's issue retells Thor's fishing expedition with Hymir, in which he hooked the serpent. The Midgard Serpent returned to plague Thor several more times in storylines that are not drawn from Norse sources.

From October 1962, two months after Thor's debut, Marvel writers began weaving the realm of Asgard and its inhabitants into the world of their comics. Many other characters and creatures were drawn from Norse myth, including Odin (debut October 1962), Surtur (October 1963), Thor's wife Sif (March 1964), and a Valkyrie named Brunnhilde (December 1970).

A Thor's Hammer pendant from Bredsättra, Öland, Sweden. (PD-US)

Actor Chris Hemsworth as the Marvel Comics Thor in the 2011 movie.
(Photos 12 / Alamy)

In the Marvel universe, Asgard is a planetoid and the Asgardians, although not immortal, are extremely long-lived. They are also physically stronger and tougher than humans. In most other respects, though, Marvel departs very little from Norse lore. Given the similarities between the tall tales of the *Eddas* and the modern superhero genre, it might be argued that there is very little reason to do so.

Thor's legacy seems destined to endure. As befits a Viking role model, he embodies an old Norse proverb about what is truly important in life:

> Cattle die, kinfolk die; everyone dies in the end. Only one thing lives forever, and that is fame.

GLOSSARY

Adam of Bremen (Latin: *Adamus Bremensis*): An 11th-century German chronicler who describes a temple of Thor at Uppsala in Sweden.

Aegir: A giant or sea god who held a feast for the Aesir.

Aesir: One of two tribes of Norse gods. Odin and Thor were prominent Aesir.

Alvis: A cunning dwarf who tries to woo Thor's daughter but is outwitted.

Asatru: A revived form of Norse paganism: literally "Aesir faith."

Asgard: The realm of the Aesir.

Balder: The fairest of the Aesir, killed by a jealous Loki.

Bifrost: A rainbow bridge connecting Asgard and Midgard.

Bilskirnir: "Lightning-crack," one of Thor's three residences.

Blot: A pagan Norse festival.

Brokk and Sindri: Two dwarves who made many of the Aesir's magical treasures.

Codex Regius: A manuscript containing most of the *Poetic Edda*. See *Eddas*.

Donar: An early Germanic name for Thor.

Eddas: Two books, one in verse and one in prose, preserving much of surviving Norse mythology.

Einherjar: Warriors who die well in battle and are chosen by the Valkyries to be taken to Valhalla.

Mjolnir by Miguel Coimbra

Elli: A servant of Utgardaloki, actually a personification of age.

Eyrbyggja Saga: An account of a feud in Viking-age Iceland. Includes a description of a Norse temple.

Fenrir: A huge wolf, the offspring of Loki, who kills Odin at Ragnarok. Also called Fenris.

Fimbulvetr: "The Great Winter," a winter lasting three years that precedes Ragnarok.

Flateyarbok: A late 14th-century account of various Norse kings.

Flyting: A bloodless duel conducted by exchanging insults.

Freyja: The most beautiful of the Norse goddesses, a patron of love and fertility.

Frigga: The wife of Odin and mother of Balder.

Geirrod: A giant who tries to murder Thor.

Gjallarhorn: The horn with which Heimdall raises the alarm when Asgard is attacked at Ragnarok.

Gridarvolr: An iron staff lent to Thor by Gridr.

Gridr: A giantess who helps Thor against Geirrod.

Harbard: A rude ferryman encountered by Thor; possibly Odin in disguise.

Heimdall: An Aesir who kept watch over the rainbow bridge Bifrost.

Heimskringla: A 13th-century collection of Old Norse kings' sagas.

Hel: The gloomy land of the dead and the goddess who rules over it.

Hod: A blind god whom Loki tricks into killing Balder.

Hrungnir: A boastful giant whom Thor killed in a duel.

Hugi: A servant of Utgardaloki, actually a personification of thought.

Hymir: A giant who was the father of the god Tyr.

Idun: A goddess whose golden apples kept the Aesir from aging.

Jarl: A Norse noble. The name is related to the Anglo-Saxon *eorl* and modern English *earl.*

Jarngreipr: Thor's magical iron gloves.

Jormungand: The name of the Midgard Serpent.

Jotun: Giants.

Jotunheim: The realm of the giants.

Landnamabok: An account of the Viking settlement of Iceland.

Logi: A servant of Utgardaloki, actually a personification of fire.

Loki: The trickster god of the Norse pantheon.

Magni: Thor's son, the strongest of the Norse gods.

Megingjord: Thor's magical belt of strength.

Midgard: The realm of mortals. The name can be translated as "Middle-earth."

Midgard Serpent: A vast serpent that lay under the sea, encircling the realm of Midgard.

Mimir: The wisest of the Aesir, whose severed head is consulted for its wisdom.

Mjolnir: Thor's mighty hammer. Also spelled Mjölnir, Mjollnir, Mjölner or Mjølner. A few sources describe Mjolnir as an axe or club rather than a hammer.

Muspelheim: The realm of the Fire Giants.

Naglfari: A ship made of dead men's nails, which will convey the hordes of Hel or the giants to Asgard at Ragnarok.

Niflheim: The realm of the Frost Giants.

Odin: Thor's father and the leader of the Aesir.

Old Uppsala (Swedish: *Gamla Uppsala*): An important political and religious center in Viking-age Sweden, the site of a major pagan temple described by Adam of Bremen.

Ragnarok: The end of the current age according to Norse myth.

The Thor I booster was used by NASA in the 1950s. NASA photograph. (Library of Congress)

Rast: An old Norse measure of distance, equivalent to 7.018 miles.

Rus: Swedish Vikings (the name may be derived from Old Swedish *ruotsi*: "rowers") who traveled east up northern Europe's great rivers, giving their name to Russia, serving the Byzantine Emperor of Constantinople and encountering Muslim travelers in the Black Sea region.

Sald: An old Norse measure of volume, about 22 gallons.

Sif: A goddess, the wife of Thor.

Sigfusson, Saemund: A 12th-century Icelandic priest credited (though not unanimously) with authorship of the *Poetic Edda* (see *Eddas*).

Skrymir: A name used by the giant Utgardaloki to trick Thor.

Sleipnir: Odin's magical eight-legged horse.

Sturluson, Snorri: A 13th-century Icelandic scholar who preserved most of the surviving Norse myths in the *Prose Edda* (see *Eddas*).

Surtur: The king of the Fire Giants.

Tanngrisnir and Tanngnjostr: Two goats that pulled Thor's chariot.

Thjalfi: A farmer's son who became Thor's servant and companion.

Thrudheim: "World of Strength," one of Thor's three residences.

Thrudvang: "Field of Power," one of Thor's three residences.

Thule Society: A secret society founded in 1911 for the study of Germanic religion and tradition. Some of its members became leaders in the Nazi Party.

Thunor: An Anglo-Saxon name for Thor.

Thunaer: A name for Thor used in the 9th century in Germany.

Thrym: A giant who stole Thor's hammer Mjolnir.

Tryggvason, Olaf: A king of Norway, later a saint, who worked to establish Christianity in his country.

Viking Revival: A 19th-century Romantic movement in Scandinavia and Germany marked by a resurgence of interest in Norse mythology and culture.

Tyr: The Aesir god of the law.

Utgard: The realm of Utgardaloki. Literally "outlands."

Utgardaloki: A giant (in some versions the king of the Jotun) who tricks Thor and Loki with several illusions.

Valhalla: Odin's hall in Asgard.

Valkyries: Goddesses who roam the battlefields choosing those who died well and conducting them to Valhalla.

Vanir: The second, and lesser-known, tribe of Norse gods, to whom Frey and Freyja belonged.

Yggdrasil: The great ash-tree that binds together all the worlds of Norse cosmogony.

FOR MORE INFORMATION

The American-Scandinavian Foundation (ASF)
Scandinavia House
58 Park Avenue
New York, NY 10016
(212) 779-3587
Website: http://www.amscan.org
The American-Scandinavian Foundation is a nonprofit organization that
    promotes exchange between the United States and the Nordic
    countries (Denmark, Finland, Iceland, Norway, and Sweden) through
    fellowships, grants, and internships. It hosts exhibitions, films, and
    concerts at its headquarters, Scandinavia House, in New York, NY.

Anti-Defamation League (ADL)
605 3rd Avenue
New York, NY 10158
(212) 885-7700
Website: http://www.adl.org
Founded in 1913, the Anti-Defamation League fights anti-Semitism and
    advocates for justice and civil rights for everyone. The ADL warns that
    neo-Nazi and white supremacist groups have co-opted the symbol
    of Thor's hammer, though the hammer is also an icon for non-racist
    groups, such as certain pagan religions.

Association for the Advancement of Scandinavian Studies in Canada (AASSC)
University of Alberta
116 Street and 85 Avenue
Edmonton, AB T6G 2R3
Canada
(780) 679-1573
Website: http://www.aassc.com
The AASSC works with the Canadian Institute for Nordic Studies at
    the University of Alberta to promote interdisciplinary research
    on Scandinavian culture. The group publishes a journal, hosts an
    annual conference, and bestows scholarships for both graduate and
    undergraduate students to study in Nordic countries.

Nordic Heritage Museum
3014 NW 67th Street
Seattle, WA 98117

(206) 789-5707
Website: https://www.nordicmuseum.org
In addition to its exhibits, the Nordic Heritage Museum sponsors many
events and education programs showcasing Nordic stories, art, crafts,
song, and dance.

Scandinavian East Coast Museum
440 Ovington Avenue
Brooklyn, NY 11209
(718) 748-5950
Website: http://www.scandinavian-museum.org
The Scandinavian East Coast Museum sponsors an annual Viking Fest to
celebrate Viking music, dance, and cuisine. The organization also
participates in other cultural events and has a virtual museum of
artifacts that commemorate Scandinavian immigration to the United
States.

University of Wisconsin-Madison
Department of Scandinavian Studies
1306 Van Hise Hall
1220 Linden Drive
Madison, WI 53705
(608) 262-2090
Website: http://scandinavian.wisc.edu
The University of Wisconsin-Madison boasts the oldest department of
Scandinavian studies in North America. It offers courses in literature,
folklore, modern Scandinavian languages, and Old Norse, as well as
study abroad opportunities.

WEBSITES

Because of the changing nature of Internet links, Rosen Publishing has
developed an online list of websites related to the subject of this book. This
site is updated regularly. Please use this link to access this list:

http://www.rosenlinks.com/HERO/Thor

FOR FURTHER READING

Brown, Nancy Marie. *Song of the Vikings: Snorri and the Making of Norse Myths*. New York, NY: Palgrave Macmillan, 2012.

Colum, Padraic. *The Children of Odin: The Book of Northern Myths*. Oxford, England: Benediction Classics, 2011.

Daly, Kathleen N. *Norse Mythology A to Z*. 3rd ed. New York, NY: Facts on File, 2009.

Denton, Shannon Eric. *Thor* (Short Tales: Norse Myths). Minneapolis, MN: Magic Wagon, 2010.

Gaiman, Neil. *American Gods*. 10th anniversary edition. New York, NY: William Morrow, 2013.

Green, Roger Lancelyn. *Myths of the Norsemen*. Reprint edition. New York, NY: Puffin Classics, 2013.

Hamby, Zachary. *Reaching Valhalla: Tales and Sagas from Norse Mythology*. Hamby Publishing, 2013.

Hamilton, Edith. *Mythology: Timeless Tales of Gods and Heroes*. Reprint edition. New York, NY: Grand Central Publishing, 2011.

Hoena, Blake. *Everything Mythology*. Des Moines, IA: National Geographic Children's Books, 2014.

Jeffrey, Gary. *Giants* (Graphic Mythical Creatures). New York, NY: Gareth Stevens Publishing, 2012.

Lee, Stan. *Thor: Tales of Asgard*. New York, NY: Marvel Comics, 2011.

Lindow, John. *Norse Mythology: A Guide to Gods, Heroes, Rituals, and Beliefs*. New York, NY: Oxford University Press, 2002.

Ollhoff, Jim. *Norse Mythology* (The World of Mythology). Minneapolis, MN: ABDO, 2011.

Philip, Neil. *Eyewitness Mythology*. Revised edition. London, England: DK Publishing, 2011.

Porterfield, Jason. *Scandinavian Mythology* (Mythology Around the World). New York, NY: Rosen Publishing, 2008.

Sigfusson, Saemund. *The Poetic Edda*. Trans. Carolyne Larrington. Reissue edition. Oxford, England: Oxford University Press, 2008.

Sturluson, Snorri. *The Prose Edda*. Trans. Jesse L. Byock. New York, NY: Penguin Classics, 2005.

Tacitus. *Agricola and Germania*. Trans. Harold Mattingly. New York, NY: Penguin Classics, 2010.

Tacitus. *The Annals*. Trans. Cynthia Damon. New York, NY: Penguin Classics, 2013.

Vasich, Mike. *Loki: Nine Naughty Tales of the Trickster*. CreateSpace, 2012.

INDEX